Conversations
with the

Dream
Mentor

About the Author

Von Braschler (Minnesota) is a former editor and publisher of community newspapers and magazines. He is a lifetime member of the Theosophical Society, and he has led workshops on energetic healing, meditation, and Kirlian photography. He is a certified message therapist specializing in pet massage.

To Write to the Author

If you wish to contact the author or would like more information about this book, please write to the author in care of Llewellyn Worldwide and we will forward your request. Both the author and publisher appreciate hearing from you and learning of your enjoyment of this book and how it has helped you. Llewellyn Worldwide cannot guarantee that every letter written to the author can be answered, but all will be forwarded. Please write to:

Von Braschler
℅ Llewellyn Worldwide
P.O. Box 64383, Dept. 0-7387-0250-1
St. Paul, MN 55164-0383, U.S.A.
Please enclose a self-addressed stamped envelope for reply,
or $1.00 to cover costs. If outside U.S.A., enclose
international postal reply coupon.

Many of Llewellyn's authors have websites with additional information and resources. For more information, please visit our website at:
http://www.llewellyn.com

Conversations
with the
Dream
Mentor

✣

Awaken to Your Inner Guide

VON BRASCHLER

2003
Llewellyn Publications
St. Paul, Minnesota 55164-0383, U.S.A.

First Edition
First Printing, 2003

Book design by Michael Maupin
Cover art © 2003 by Neal Armstrong / Koralik Associates
Cover design by Llewellyn Art Department

Library of Congress Cataloging-in-Publication Data
Braschler, Von, 1947–
    Conversations with the dream mentor : awaken to your inner guide / Von
    Braschler.—1st ed.
      p.   cm.
    ISBN 0-7387-0250-1
    1. Astral projection. 2. Guides (Spiritualism) I. Title: Dream mentor. II. Title.

    BF1389.A7B2 2003
    131—dc21   2002043319

Llewellyn Publications
A Division of Llewellyn Worldwide, Ltd.
P.O. Box 64383, Dept. 0-7387-0250-1
St. Paul, MN 55164-0383, U.S.A.
www.llewellyn.com

Printed in the United States of America

Also by Von Braschler

Perfect Timing:
Mastering Time Perception for Personal Excellence

Dedicated to Mari,
who helped me find the magic in life.

The author will donate personal profits
from the sale of this book to
charities for animal shelters
and wildlife preserves.

Thank you for helping
make this possible!

Contents

Introduction

I FIRST MET my dream mentor in 1980 when I lived in a cabin in the woods on a snowy mountaintop in Oregon. Actually, I was introduced to him and presented to him for supplemental training of a very personal nature. Because this training was so personalized and because my access to the dream mentor was through altered states of consciousness during meditation and lucid dreaming, I have been reluctant to disclose my conversations with him. These conversations were simply too intimate to discuss, I thought. Also, these meetings with the dream mentor were always in a nonphysical world, visited in a dream state or meditative state.

Then I discovered that many other people have experienced lessons taught by a dream mentor similar to my experience. Indeed, many mystics from both the East and the West have described receiving esoteric instruction in a dream state from a teacher who sounds and apparently resembles my own dream mentor. I know, for instance, that followers of Eckankar (soul travel to reach the divine) and Sethians (readers of Jane Roberts books on alternate realities) believe in dreaming with mysterious dream teachers to learn esoteric truths. Native American shamans for years have explored the dream world where they would receive esoteric lessons of a personal nature from dream teachers. The same is true of Hindu mystics.

In addition, many people have described going to a mysterious teaching room in their dreams. There they encounter other dreamers who gather in a sort of circle and sit upon the ground. The room is generally described the same in these accounts. There are doors leading out from the circular teaching room. Sometimes the people in these dream classrooms observe clothing of the people who attend as simple tunics or robes, often white in color. Then a teacher enters through one of the doors and quietly walks to the center of the room ringed by students. He is often described as older, short of stature, a bit stout, and dressed in a simple white tunic or robe. He speaks to the entire group, but seems to say something different to each student at the same time. He is a dream mentor, a master.

In all of these accounts, the dreamer enters a mysterious realm or plane of existence that is clearly not of this ordinary world. In all of these accounts, the dreamer is instantly put in front of a teaching master who answers whatever questions are foremost in the dreamer's mind, often with cryptic or esoteric responses. Most curiously, the dream mentor appears again and again to the dreamer in much the same fashion, often establishing a fixed setting for the esoteric instruction. Most descriptions of the dream mentor sound much the same in all of these accounts.

Consequently, the dream mentor appears to us as a universal archetype. He is universally available to us as an archetype that can be accessed in states of higher consciousness.

I believe I would have trouble with this concept of a personal dream mentor being a universal archetype if I had not met the renowned psychic Louis Gittner, author of *Love Is a Verb* and *Listen, Listen, Listen.* In addition to running his Louis Foundation, his Outlook Inn resort, and writing books on spiritual growth through meditation, Louis Gittner maintains one of the most beautiful and astounding gardens I have ever seen. The gardens surround his inn on Orcas Island, Washington state, in the San Juans. Everything that grows there seems to be in robust health and huge in size. Among the things Louis has grown in his gardens are vegetables for the inn, including prized peas.

Apparently, however, Louis Gittner has received special instructions on peas from the spirit world. Gittner through the years has always received special communications from the spirit world while reclining in a meditative state in much the same repose as the sleeping prophet, Edgar Cayce.

Gittner told me during my visit to his inn how he received information about the peas in his garden on Orcas Island, Washington, at exactly the same time one of the founders of Findhorn received precisely the same information about garden peas. Gittner said he visited the famed Findhorn gardens in Scotland where everything grew perfectly to enormous size to determine whether the founders' special rapport with the nature kingdom was similar to his own advice from nonphysical entities. He began to wonder whether the special communication which he received was similar to the communication received at the Findhorn gardens in Scotland. So he visited Findhorn and compared his diary. Amazingly, the information he received on peas at a specific time and date was the same as the information received on peas at Findhorn gardens at that exact same time and date. That even accounts for the different time zones. So communications of this sort can happen simultaneously to more than one person miles apart.

Obviously, there are universal archetypes at work and accessible to people who can find a way to communicate with them. The Findhorn deva of the pea is certainly one universal archetype who speaks to many people who would seek her out. The dream mentor who visits with people in their profound dreams and offers insight is perhaps another universal archetype. It would seem that many people can contact such a dream mentor at the same time and access him for personal assistance.

The personal encounter with the dream mentor is highly interactive and can be exhausting. The dream mentor will stretch your imagination and tax your endurance. He will challenge you at times. Nothing worth learning or having comes easily, he seems to be saying.

In recounting my own experiences and lessons with my dream mentor, I can see a startling similarity to many such accounts in the very private and mysterious encounters that I have had with a dream mentor throughout the years. As a mystic, I can only believe my own experiences and trust them to be the truth, as I have personally experienced it. I know and trust no other reality. Therefore, I wish to share my personal experiences with my dream mentor in the belief that this teacher on a non-ordinary plane of consciousness is a universal archetype that others can meet.

These true stories, told in the first person, will give you real insights into the sorts of adventures and lessons that await you in dream teaching and the approach a dream mentor will take in introducing metaphysical truths and mysteries of life to you. Of course, this encounter will be slightly different for you, shaded by your personal needs and particular interests. The dream mentor will tailor your lessons especially for you in a way that connects best with you. Also, your analysis of the way the dream mentor looks, communicates, or introduces you to subjects will be filtered through your own, unique perception that is colored by your own sphere of reference and orientation.

Everyone is a little different; and the skillful dream mentor takes all of that into careful consideration in teaching you. The settings and topics selected for your conversations with the dream mentor, however, will be your own choosing. You pick the topics and the classroom basically. The dream mentor will be waiting there for you, when you are ready to discuss and explore your deepest questions and mysteries.

So my own conversations with the dream mentor are offered here only as examples of the sort of exploration that you can have when you connect with the dream mentor on your own. If you study the conversations that I have had with the dream mentor, you also will get some idea how to relate to the dream mentor and how to react in the active dream state that will take you to distant worlds of discovery. Consequently, my personal conversations and adventures with the dream mentor are not meant to be entertaining stories, but rather a format or template for your own conversations with the dream mentor. Your lessons will be unique to you, but the format for approaching the dream mentor for these dream lessons will be basically the same for everyone.

Techniques for reaching the meditative level of consciousness that is required to meet the dream mentor are presented at the back of this book. Consequently, this book could be read as a "how to" book on how to personally contact a dream mentor.

You will not find this mysterious master anywhere on this physical earth, as far as I can see. You can only reach him by raising your consciousness and establishing with him a desire for help. He will know when you are ready. The sort of questions that he will entertain and answer for you are somewhat deeper than petty concerns about personal gains. He will not, for instance, answer questions about winning lottery numbers, your best times for travel, or whether you should marry a certain person.

Some of the stories in this book might give you ideas about what sort of questions he will entertain. Certainly, he appears fascinated with the true nature of things, the order of things in the universe, personal spiritual growth, and the evolution of human potential. I also have noticed that he teaches with overt description, often acting out the answer to a deep riddle, so that the answer becomes obvious—although often hard to put into words.

It is important to distinguish, too, that contacts with the dream mentor are not in any way related to channeling, mediums, automatic writing, trance states, or spirit possession. These are profound, personal dreams that people have been experiencing for years. The belief in the revelatory power of dream teaching is at least as old as the Bible. King David of the Jews, according to that holy book, had revelatory dreams in which he learned answers to perplexing, personal questions. Indeed, people for years have put great faith in answers to tough questions in their dreams.

But how do you experience such a dream that will put you in touch with answers to your deepest, personal questions? And how do you establish contact with a dream teacher?

This book will show you how to put yourself in such a special dream state and how to contact a dream mentor.

One

Contacting a Dream Mentor

DESCRIBING HOW TO contact a dream mentor and what to expect demands a first-person approach, I think. After all, it's a mystical experience. Therefore, a mystical approach to gathering knowledge is probably best. A mystic relies on experience in gathering knowledge, whereas a purely academic scholar relies generally on empirical knowledge from an overwhelming body of outside, impartial sources of information to make a case. I can only report my case and faithfully relay the actual case history of my own encounters in contacting and relating to a dream mentor.

This is a teaching master who visits you in your sleep or meditations and takes you to exotic realms for profound lessons on the nature of things, the order of the universe, and the purpose and potential of human living. I have learned to trust these encounters as valuable and meaningful, as I put them into practical use in my life and worldview.

If you are able to follow the outline of procedures described in this text and itemized in step-by-step exercises at the back of this book, then you also might access the universal archetype known to many as the dream mentor or master. This is not a dangerous encounter, since the dream mentor I have come to know personally is not a tyrant, lord, demon, or dominating leader who will command you to follow his rule or teachings. Rather, he is a gentle and patient teacher who suggests answers to your most basic, yet profound questions about the nature of things. He lets you pose the question to him. If he considers it an important question—not something trivial or petty, then he acts out the problem and solution for you in rather dramatic fashion. What you do with this profound, basic truth is totally up to you in your exercise of free will and choice.

My first encounter with the dream mentor happened around 1980 when I was living in a cabin in the woods beside the Salmon River on Mount Hood in Oregon. It was a place known as Brightwood, so named by Native Americans who used to spend summers in these beautiful, sleepy woods. I was publisher of the local newspaper at the time and pre-occupied most of the day with the gathering of hard facts and news. When I moved to that part of Oregon, I did not realize that Mount Hood was an active volcano that rumbled almost as much as did its twin peak, Mount Saint Helens, across the neighboring Columbia River. Also, I did not real-ize that earlier settlers not so long ago had lost their homes along the river bank, due to periodic flooding from the glacier-fed Salmon River.

One year, when the area lost all power due to a blizzard that froze our pipes and imprisoned us in our homes, I learned the inner peace and sublime tranquility the area offered. It was a chance to learn again how to live in harmony with nature and get in contact with my inner self. I spent days alone in my dark cabin, making candles and meditating dur-ing the day and then burning logs that had dried all day for the quiet evenings. I learned to utilize the woods as my restroom and bath in the icy river by hanging on to a tree limb by shore.

I used all of the shoelaces in my closet to make candles. Each day, my limited supply of wax would burn down, so that I would need to make a new candle for the next day. The candles afforded me the luxury of read-ing all of those great self-improvement books that I had never taken the time to read.

When it started to get dark and my candle burned down, I would meditate. Then I would go to bed early, usually still in a meditative state. In a sense, I was living as the ancients lived before modern conveniences. I lived by the sun and moon and utilized the woods and river as part of my daily life.

I had books on meditation, color magic, chant, and tone. I also had books on astral projection, self-hypnosis, imagery, and consciousness training. In the past, I had attended meetings in the Portland area sponsored by the Berkeley Psychic Institute, Eckankar International, and others. But I had always been too busy to read or practice anything I had learned to any significant degree. To practice these esoteric principles, you need time to yourself. The storm that kept me snowbound in my cabin in the woods for a week without groceries or human contact gave me all of the time I needed to explore this world of esoteric truth and heightened consciousness.

I honestly don't believe that I ever would have met the dream master or learned the techniques required to access that level of consciousness without first learning how to meditate, visualize, and leave my body. Many readers might find these concepts a bit far-fetched. I would hasten to point out, however, that shamans, Hindu mystics, and other spirit walkers have been doing these sorts of things for ages. The only difference is that they have practiced in quiet solitude with the time and patience required to access these levels of nonordinary reality. In my case, it took a long snowstorm and a dark, empty house to push me to that point. Now, I'm really glad that it snowed.

I would meditate late in the day, before the sun went down and I went to bed. My approach to meditation was based largely on previous study of self-hypnosis. In both meditation and self-hypnosis, a person *wills* the physical body and its senses to become numb. In a real sense, the physical body is told to go to sleep. The mind, however, stays awake and active.

The idea is to shut off all external distractions and your sensory overload of smell, taste, hearing, seeing, and feeling. You want to cease processing this sort of sensory information. In addition, you want to still your inner voice and cease internal dialogue. This means shutting down the endless loop of random thoughts that all people play over and over in their minds. Usually this involves your pressing concerns over matters of the past or worries about the future. You need to clear your mind of all such internal chatter in order to enter a state of superconsciousness—

the goal of both self-hypnosis and meditation. It's also important to be comfortable, but grounded during this process. You might want to try sitting on a chair or on the floor in an erect position. Remember, the body grows numb and the mind is emptied on all distractions both externally and internally. The mind is then freed to assume a new role with total focus. The mind becomes keenly alert and enters a state of superconsciousness and heightened awareness.

Here is where hypnosis and meditation usually part company to a degree. In hypnosis, the mind is then probed by a hypnotist and led through a series of suggestions. Sometimes a hypnotist in therapy sessions will give a subject a post-hypnotic suggestion to do something in a key situation in the future. On the other hand, meditators enter a state of heightened consciousness and let their minds stretch to explore beyond the bodily restraints of this physical world and ordinary reality. The meditator, then, is on a journey of self-discovery in a sense, whereas the hypnosis subject generally is being assisted by a therapist who directs the subject through a certain pattern of deep thoughts.

I'm so glad that I learned self-hypnosis, before I really tried to meditate seriously. All of those little meditation inducements such as dots on walls, chants, and bells really didn't put me into a deep trance that took me on any great journey of self-discovery. Like a lot of people, it just made me relaxed and quiet for a little while, until I became bored from just sitting there and doing nothing. I kept feeling all the time as though I were really missing something—like the whole point of it. Meditation, after all, is meant to be active participation, not just quiet repose and introspection.

Self-hypnosis helped me learn how to really meditate, however, and eventually took me on great journeys of self-discovery where I met the dream mentor and worlds beyond worlds. And all it took to get me started was a little post-hypnotic suggestion before I trotted off to bed.

I would also gaze into my candle, so a little candle magic must have been involved. At least the candle helped me focus in the beginning and helped me lose myself in the moment. In serious meditation, it's important to fix yourself solidly in the moment and forget about the future and the past.

Part of my little post-hypnotic suggestion as I put myself to bed was to visualize colors. These were flashing, bright colors that acted as a sort of beacon for me. I would lie on my back in a state of heightened consciousness and half close my eyes, so that light would enter through my eyelashes. Then I would transform the color of the light into yellow light. Next I would visualize the light becoming orange. Then I would visualize red light and try to control the intensity of the red so that it would range from a light red to a deep red. At last, I would visualize a rapid succession of changing color bursts, ranging from yellow to orange to red. I would continue this kaleidoscope process of color visualization until I saw only black at the end.

The blackness that I saw was the void of the conscious realm, a world beyond the physical. Out of blackness, all things come. The blackness of space and time leads to all worlds and all realms. It holds the full potential of all creation. From there all things come. Unrestricted by the physical limitations of a dense body and the limited sensory observations of that body, a soul can travel anywhere. It's the doorway to spirit and the vast, unlimited domains of unexplored worlds within worlds.

This, then, became my goal. I wanted to explore the nonphysical worlds through heightened attention. In putting myself into a meditative state with a post-hypnotic suggestion, I was willing myself to leave my body.

I quickly learned, however, that leaving the body can be as painful as being born and leaving the comfort of the womb. You need to plan for an easy escape. Eastern mystics suggest options, often relating to the seven major chakra centers or energy vortexes vertically aligned in the body. Carlos Castaneda wrote that his sorcery teacher in Mexico whacked him on the lower back, once he was properly aligned and ready. I didn't have anyone in my snowstorm to whack me on the back.

So I experimented. I quickly learned that leaving the body through the head's brow chakra or crown chakra felt painful. What worked best for me was for my consciousness to leave my physical body through the lower abdomen.

The first time I did this I found myself suddenly floating in darkness. I couldn't focus on anything. It's almost as though I needed a new kind of vision to see my way in this nonphysical world outside the body. Also, I sort of panicked and quickly returned to my body. Well, it had been my comfort and my haven for all of my physical life. The new worlds were strange to me; and I had no training or guide.

Returning to the physical body in a panic creates a sudden snapping sensation in that part of that body where you exited. In my case, I ended up with a flash of confusing blackness, followed almost instantly by a tummy ache.

Then I got lucky. After putting myself into an state of heightened awareness one night, I walked into the bedroom and flopped down on the bed to begin my visualization exercises. I always reclined on my back and squinted my eyes in the dim light of dusk to try to leave my body through my lower abdomen. Only this time, I landed awkwardly on the bed, striking my lower back against the hard edge of the bed.

Instantly, the pain gripped me and I blacked out for an instant. Then I felt my conscious self quickly evacuating my body. It seemed as though my life essence sensed that my physical body had suddenly died or become an unsafe vessel. Perhaps this is what athletes feel when they get the air suddenly kicked out of them or what near-death experiences are all about. Maybe it's what the Kirlians in their near-death experiments observed in electrocuting the body of subjects to measure weight loss as their life essence momentarily left their bodies.

In my case, I was fully conscious and alert, yet I saw only blackness. I wondered for a second whether I was unconscious or simply unable to see. My uncertainly lasted only an instant. Suddenly I could see the room around me; however, everything looked a little hazy. I had the sensation then that I was floating in the air. I looked down and saw the bed with my body lying on the bed. So I naturally wondered how I could be looking at myself down on the bed and yet be in another place at the same time. Then I fully realized that I had left my body.

At last, everything seemed fine and comfortable to me. I felt a surge of joy and peace, and I wanted to sing out. I felt free—totally free, in a way I had never felt before. I let go of all inhibitions. I floated higher above the bed until I reached the very top of the roof. I continued to look down at my limp body flopped on the bed, faceup. I looked so peaceful on that bed, so happy.

I rose higher and suddenly found myself outside the house, looking down at the snow-covered rooftop. I rose yet higher and saw the boughs of majestic evergreen trees and smoke curling from my chimney. I floated to the top of the mammoth evergreens and looked at their ninety-foot peaks. The house below seemed smaller to me now. I felt a strange disinterest in the little house below and the man flopped on the bed inside the tiny, snow-covered house. I felt removed from the situation below me.

Then it hit me. I started to panic. How could I just leave my body behind? What if I could not get back into my body? Would I die? What would become of that part of me that was floating in the treetops? What would I do? What of the future?

Then I felt a sudden jolt in my abdomen and found myself rolling on the bed inside the house. I opened my eyes and saw the ceiling of the dimly lit house. I felt the awkward edge of the bed against my lower back and shifted to a more comfortable position on the bed.

Darn! I had left my body and traveled through the night sky, but couldn't deal with it! I had panicked and started to worry about my body. I had fretted about the future. None of these things are real concerns in the nonordinary world of higher consciousness. These are only concerns of the mundane world.

The next day I analyzed my first real out-of-body experience and its shortcomings. It occurred to me that I'd had no plan, goal, or direction once I left my body. I did not know what to do or where to do it. I was just floating around, observing myself from above. That seemed like a silly waste of a fine opportunity. But, honestly, I had no idea where to go or what to do. I did not know how to go anywhere. What was out there in the great unknown? I had read something about it, but had no practical guide to proceed. I was in uncharted territories, as far as I was concerned. It seemed daunting to me to just strike out alone in the great void. It seemed too dark. I had no sense that I could control my direction from my first out-of-body experience, which was actually a freak accident.

The only movement that I had experienced in my spirited adventure that first evening was a sort of upward floating sensation. It seemed that I had willed myself to continue the ascent, however. So I seemed to have some control in this altered state of reality, but not a lot of direction.

How could I get some sense of direction? I wanted to have an out-of-body experience again. But if I could, would it be any more meaningful? There had to be more to it than simply drifting aimlessly in the night sky and looking down at my body and house below. That was an amazing trick, to be sure, but not the sort of astral travel or soul voyage that I had imagined would take me to exotic realms of alternate realities. Where were these other worlds of reality beyond the physical world? That, to me, seemed the only great use of this out-of-body travel. My higher consciousness had just hovered over my little cabin in the woods, much the same way stinky smoke lingers over a greasy grill at a wayside diner.

My cat, Sleepy, had watched the whole ordeal and now was giving me funny looks. In typical cat arrogance, she seemed to be say, "What's wrong with you? Can't you get it right?" It should be pointed out that Sleepy spent half of her life on that same bed and a good deal of the rest of the time reclining on my sofa. Now I was beginning to wonder whether such an alert and adventuresome creature as my cat really *slept* 16–20 hours every day. Maybe she wasn't sleeping all of that time.

I was determined to try leaving my body again and determined to do it better this time. The previous night's adventure had been a big breakthrough for me. I couldn't stop now.

So I decided to give myself a very specific post-hypnotic suggestion. As I drifted into an out-of-body state next time, I would focus on calling for some sort of guide to lead the way. My next opportunity came that very night.

I meditated in my usual manner, except that I gave myself this extra special, post-hypnotic suggestion. I walked up to the bedroom, still in a state of heightened consciousness. I lay on my back upon the bed, resting the small of my back uncomfortably on the hard edge of the bed that had shocked me out of my body the night before. I figured that my body would remember, and that nudge in the right place on my lower spine would trigger an easy release from my body. Then I half-closed my eyes and began seeing the bright yellow, orange, and red colors pulsating. I was mesmerized by the kaleidoscope of colors. At last, the rotating colors disappeared, replaced by black—absolute darkness inside my head. Then the post-hypnotic suggestion kicked in. I called out for a guide in the blackness.

Suddenly a hand reached out and grabbed me in the darkness. It pulled me forward with a lunge. I was ripped out of the bedroom and out of the house in an instant. Then I sensed that we were racing through the night sky. What a rush!

My vision became crystal clear for the first time; and I saw the stars in the night. We were moving so quickly that the stars seemed to streak by us. I looked at the person who held my hand. It was a young woman in a light, flowing gown. She was slender with long, dark hair.

This guide seemed to be a gentle spirit. She smiled at me for a moment, but did not speak. Her attention turned back to the sky ahead, as though she were navigating her way through the vast expanse of space.

When she thought she had gone far enough, she brought us down to the ground very gracefully. She seemed to know where she was going. It was a sort of factory or plant of some sort, with all glass windows and glass doors. Still holding my hand gently, she walked us inside.

I looked at her. She appeared to be a young woman of approximately twenty-seven years old. I would guess that she looked to be about 5'7" tall with medium, dark hair halfway down her back. I guessed it to be brown, but really couldn't distinguish colors other than light and dark. She appeared thin, with excellent posture and carriage. Her eyes were dark and piercing. She wore a simple, flowing gown of light color. Most remarkably, she seemed to look right through me. She motioned with the hand that was not holding on to mine for me to look around the building we had entered.

It was all glass-enclosed and overlooked a room below. Everywhere I glanced around the building, I saw tubes and tables filled with tubes. These tubes were dark in color and made of something like rubber or plastic, with the impression of elasticity. The tables appeared to be work tables. Anything could be made here, I thought, by stretching and fitting these elastic tubes together. We walk together to the edge of the room and looked over railings down at a room below. There was a huge, glass partition at the edge of the room, so that you could either look down at the room below or the sky above. The room below looked something like a warehouse or assembly plant with more tubes of various sizes. I saw no other people in this building.

I thought that it was strange I seemed to have a body myself, since it was only my consciousness that had made the journey there. But it seemed right. I think I arranged everything I saw and experienced into comfortable forms that I could relate to. I had no frame of reference for the things I was seeing in this nonordinary reality.

I looked down at my guide's hand, as she continued to hold fast to my own. It was a soft and elegant hand with long, delicate fingers. She squeezed my hand tightly and looked deeply into my soul. She seemed to be asking what I wanted to know or do there.

It is strange that I did not hear a sound; and yet I could understand exactly what she seemed to be saying to me. The voice, if you could call it that, resonating inside my whole conscious being like a series of harmonic tones that triggered a response inside me. The voice was soft and helpful, yet abrupt in a direct sort of way. She was asking me what I wanted to learn here.

"Can you show me how to fly?" I asked her. It was the first thing that occurred to me to ask. "How do you fly?"

"Flying is easy," she said. "Anyone can fly. It's natural. But you don't do it anything like you would imagine. No wings. It's built inside of you."

She pointed to her chest and then laid one hand on my chest.

"You lead from there," she said. "Just think about moving and where you want to move and then push forward from there."

As she said this, she thrust her chest forward, as though approaching a dive off a diving board, with hands limp at her side.

"Then you just shove off," she explained.

I thrust my chest forward, with one hand still holding her hand. Together, we lifted off. We ascended through the top half of the large glass window and sailed into the sky.

This time, I seemed to propel and steer myself. Before, she had pulled me through the sky. I realized all too late that we were tugging and pulling at each other, as I seemed to be zigzagging aimlessly. I was giddy with my newfound ability to maneuver, but without any direction or plan. My guest, for the most part, seemed willing to go whatever direction I headed, although she did seem a little concern that I didn't seem to know what I was doing.

Suddenly, I found myself back in my bed, staring up at the ceiling. I rubbed my eyes. Had this all really happened? Was I asleep and just fantasizing? No, I had been in a state of heightened consciousness and alert the whole time. If it were a dream, it had been a lucid, waking dream. Everything I had seen and done was perfectly clear in great detail; and I remembered everything.

Who was this woman who guided me in my out-of-body journey? Was this what people call a guide? Or was she my guardian angel? Was she a person or a spirit? I had so many questions, and longed to meet her again to learn the answers.

The next day, I arose early and dried more damp alder on top of the wood stove for future use. After I made my new candle for the day, I bundled up for my daily constitutional walk to the river. Usually, this included a roll of toilet paper and a towel in the other hand. (My household plumbing was completely frozen and unusable still.)

Today, however, was different. I had a deeper purpose. Before my cold bath in the river, I sat on a boulder beside a white mountain ash tree. I considered this the ideal time and place to reflect on my new guide and consider who she really was.

Maybe she was my guardian angel or a spirit guide. On the other hand, she seemed like a goddess. The pagans often say that there is only one goddess in the universe, and that all manifestations of the goddess are different personalities of the same goddess. Was my guide the goddess Diana of the moon, the goddess of the woods? My understanding of the goddess Diana is that she was a sort of guardian of all living things in the forest, concerned with all creatures great and small. She was eternally young and wide-eyed.

I looked at my woodland setting beside the river and thought it most remarkable that I had sat next to a white mountain ash, which I had always believed was associated with the goddess Diana. Was this more than coincidence? Had spirit led me to sit there to learn?

I decided to test this theory. I assembled rocks to form an altar dedicated to the goddess Diana, with the white mountain ash at the top of the altar. I lay branches and pine cones on the altar and said a little prayer to the goddess. I sat on one of the boulders that faced the altar.

Frankly, I was waiting for a sign. I waited quite a while, and then felt an urge to look up into the sky. To my amazement, swirling clouds were forming shapes just a few feet above the river. They were moving quickly, despite the apparent lack of wind just a few feet below where I stood watching in wonder.

The clouds formed into the shape of a woman's face. She had long hair and a beautiful, engaging smile. She seemed to be saying "Hello" to me.

Before I could analyze the cloud image, the clouds quickly dispersed. The vision of the woman's face was erased from the sky. But I had seen it! I felt that this was a true sign. Surely, this is the nature goddess, Diana, I had seen. First, Diana comes into my mind. Then I am driven to build an altar to the goddess Diana. And as soon as the altar is built and consecrated, the vision of a goddess appears to me in the clouds. I felt convinced that I had, indeed, seen the great nature goddess. It stood to reason, therefore, that the goddess had been my guide through the nonordinary world of my vivid dreams the night before.

Convinced that I had solved a great mystery in a flash of light, I stripped off all of my clothes in the freezing snow and lowered myself into the river without uttering a single word of complaint that day. I was aglow from my vision and all smiles. I felt really loved and protected in a way that I had never felt before.

Two

Exploring Other Realms

IN ANOTHER DAY or two, the snowplows had cleared the roads and power was restored, so that I could return to work at the newspaper at the bottom of the mountain.

The journalist in me told me not to accept everything I had seen in my lucid dreams on face value and to seek outside verification. But how could I begin to verify what I had seen? Journalists rely on facts, objectivity, and credibility of sources on new information. Waking dreams with out-of-body travel would be difficult to handle in this same, calculating manner, I decided. After all, the meditative world of higher consciousness takes a person outside the physical world of normal space and time. There, the laws of physics do not apply. It is a world of personal experience. It is the world of dreams. And, after all, my dreams are simply my dreams. Certainly they would be different from another person's dreams.

Yet even my psychic teacher, Louis Gittner, the author and subject of Brad Steiger's *Words from the Source,* had cautioned against accepting every voice you might hear from the spirit realm. The reason is that you can never be totally certain who will come through to meet you and how honest they will be.

Finally, I decided that I had to determine my own reality for myself. What seemed real and right to me ultimately would form my own working version of reality, if I accepted it and acted upon it. I would simply have to determine with my own sensibility whether what I was hearing and learning in these states of altered consciousness rang true for me. As the great Indian sage J. Krishnamurti urged his many students throughout the years, I would simply need to be my own student and my own teacher and determine the truth for myself. So I vowed to keep an open mind and continue my personal odyssey of discovery.

Nothing my guide had done or said made me doubt her. She had not dominated me or forced me to do or believe anything. It seemed to me that her entire approach thus far had simply been to show me things, so that I could discover truth for myself.

So I continued to meditate and attain out-of-body dream adventures every night with my guide. She took me to many interesting places of her choosing, as though to show me things in hopes of educating me. I was tempted to ask about her to know her name and all about her, but was reluctant to press things with her. It was a magical experience for me to travel with her in the nonordinary world; and I didn't want to do anything that might change things. Asking inappropriate questions or getting too personal, I thought, might upset her or change our relationship. Also, she seemed to already know me. She acted as though I should already know her and accept her without a lot of personal, petty questions.

The emphasis in her little trips with me was always on showing me things that she wanted me to observe with a deeper understanding of the general nature of things and the relationship of things in creation. So the focus in my dream sessions with her was instructional, but filled with mystery in discovering the inner truth in things around us.

She liked to take me for walks in the woods. Perhaps it was an enchanted forest on a distant realm or level of alternate reality. It looked like a normal nature setting in any woods, however. We would walk down a path in the woods and see birds and other small, woodland creatures. She wanted me to simply walk with her and really see everything there, noting how everything reacted in its environment and interrelated. So I walked with her in silence mostly, observing fauna and flora.

She pointed out things to me along the trail and paused so that I could absorb what I had seen. I soon realized that she was looking for deeper meaning in everything we saw in those woods. She would point to an old, decaying tree along the path and then look at me for reaction, pausing long for a response. I would simply smile and tell her how much I enjoyed everything she showed me.

The woods where she took me looked like an old-growth forest. There was heavy forest canopy, so that little light reached the lower limbs and ground vegetation below. Even so, the forest glowed with a dim light that seemed to emanate internally everywhere I looked. I would guess that it was a yellowish pastel shade of luminous light, although I could still not distinguish actual colors—only shades of black and white. On the other hand, I was beginning to interpret color of light on objects, probably the same way that many aura readers can look at light energy that surrounds a human body and then internally determine the pastel shade of this light. I reasoned that this was a third-eye ability or psychic interpretation of color. It also occurred to me that everything I saw in these astral journeys had an aura.

I was beginning to believe that everything I saw in this enchanted forest was very different from the physical world I knew in my waking body. My guide quickly set me straight.

"What does this tell you?" she asked me one day, pointing to a bird sitting on an old, dead limb." She rarely spoke, so I was taken back.

"Uh, very pretty." I muttered. "I love all birds. That one seems especially beautiful."

She looked at me with a sideways stare, as though waiting for more.

"And," I rambled, "I don't think I've every seen one just like it."

Slowly, she began to walk again. I always walked slowly like this when I was trying to figure something out. Slow walks would jog my thoughts. This slow gait by my guide seemed to be that sort of deliberate, calculating walk.

I could think of nothing more pertinent or deep to say. So we just walked down the forest trail in silence. Soon I found myself back on my bed, staring at the ceiling again. It's as though I was bounced back or tossed aside.

The beauty of my relationship with my guide, however, is that I could quickly find her. Or perhaps she would find me. All I would need to do is put myself in the state of heightened consciousness through meditation and then lay on my back, fluttering my eyes to start the kaleidoscope of yellow, orange, and red colors that eventually faded to black. I no longer needed to trigger my lower back or any part of my body to leave. My body remembered how to leave. I would sense a shift in my lower spine as I would begin to see the flashing colors. Then the colors would quickly disappear, replaced by black. The next thing I would see would be my guide, standing there next to me in an exotic setting. She would just pop in front of me.

In these adventures with her, however, I began to notice how different our speech seemed in this alternate reality. It wasn't auditory at all. I didn't hear anything she said or anything I uttered in the normal manner. Then I remembered that I no longer had my ears, even though I appeared to be whole. After all, this was a nonphysical reality, a world of higher consciousness. The normal rules of the physical universe didn't apply here, because this was not a physical realm. The normal five senses that we utilize in the physical world do not come into play here. Nonetheless, I could hear whatever she said or hear myself perfectly well. It was as though I could hear inside of myself, rather than externally, as with ears. Actually, it was like hearing the thought, rather than the sound. Then I realized that we were sharing thoughts and reading each other's thoughts.

Yet I wasn't receiving her every thought, but only certain communications she intended me to receive. The same was true, it seemed, of my thoughts. She didn't seem to be responding to everything I thought; or at least she was not acting on every little thought that came to me. So it struck me that transmitted thoughts were rare and controlled by the sender in this communication process. It seemed to me that I could control this flow of outbound communications by intention and will.

Before, I had always thought of the energetic power of will as emanating from the will center in the abdominal area of the human body. Therefore, it seemed to me at first that the power to execute one's will with intentionality would be limited to the physical presence of the body. I could see now that this was not totally true. The power of will and the force to project one's intention stays with a person in a purely conscious state in astral projection of one's life essence. Our will is apparently part of our soul or spirit essence. It follows us wherever we go as a primary force at our disposal. It is like an energy force to project ourselves and our intentions.

Of course, the world of meditation through higher consciousness opens all of us to a vast, unexplored realm of new potentials, as well. It was a new realm to me, a new reality to experience. I would go there without my normal five senses, but with full consciousness. I found, too, that none of the laws of physics seemed to apply. It was, after all, a nonphysical reality. It was a spirit realm to be explored with my spirit essence. With that came my astral body (the etheric energy body that surrounds us like a glove and provides us with a health aura and an astral "double" body). It also seemed to include my soul, my "spark" of life or light body, my mental self, and my will as a projection of my life force.

In the world of out-of-body dreaming or soul travel, I felt that I had unlimited potential, since I was free of the restraints of the physical world. I was not bound to the limitations of the human body and the restrictions of its world. This was a new reality; and I was eager to explore it fully with my new capabilities.

Consequently, I was growing impatient with my kindly spirit guide to show me more and tell me more. She kept showing me the enchanted forest and pointing out birds and trees to me. I had seen birds and trees before. What could I learn from them?

And who was she, really? I did not even know her name. Because she always showed me the forest and seemed interested in giving me a deeper appreciation of nature, I assumed she was the archetype Diana, goddess of the moon and the hunt. Maybe this archetype was the same as Mother Nature or great mother of the universe. She seemed interested in all life, as a guardian or caretaker would be.

I vowed to give myself a post-hypnotic suggestion to remember to ask her name in our next meeting. So many times I seemed to forget the questions on my mind, once I entered the dream state. That seemed logical, since the dream state came upon me after clearing my mind of all concerns of the day to enter a meditative state and higher consciousness.

So the next night I approached my lucid dream with her, carrying that intent. When I suddenly appeared in front of her in the enchanted forest, she looked at me with a little surprise in her eyes. She tilted her head, as though to assess me. She seemed happily surprised that her pupil was finally ready to pose questions.

We walked for a while down the now-familiar trail in the woods and she continued to point out things that she thought should interest me. In particular, she pointed out a large, beautiful butterfly. When she pointed to the butterfly, it landed near the ground. It was almost as though the butterfly granted us an opportunity to observe it.

My guide looked at me to gauge my reaction. I had never seen anything like it before. While I still could not discern actual colors, it appeared to be yellowish. I know that I had never seen a butterfly (or whatever it was) even close to this immense size. It was quite beautiful and awesome. There were big, black dots on its enormous wings. The awesome creature sat motionless for the most part, twitching only occasionally. It allowed us to walk up to it. My guide reached out and touched it gingerly, almost reverently. Then we walked on.

I was ready to pose my question.

"What is your name?" I asked her point-blank.

She turned her head in surprise. Her dark eyes, filled with anticipation, locked onto me.

"What do you think?" she responded. "Don't you know me?"

"But I don't really. I don't even know your name."

"What do you think my name is?"

I reflected for a minute. Did she really think I already had this information inside me, like preprogramming or something? Was I born with this information? How could I know, if I hadn't been told?

Then the words just came to me, from deep inside my inner being. I scarcely recognized my own voice, if you could call it that.

"Selina," I responded. "You are Selina."

She continued to gaze at me.

"That's right?" I asked.

She just smiled.

"Am I right?" I asked her. The journalist always confirms all facts from whatever source they have come originally.

She continued to smile and walked on, with me at her side.

The next day when I first got home from work, something strange caught my eye when I walked to the back porch to switch on the porch light. I saw a huge, yellow butterfly with enormous black dots on its wings. It was simply huge, larger than anything I had ever seen—except in my dream. I rapped on the window where it clung, as though it were watching me. How could it just hang motionless on the vertical pane of glass? Was it real? Was it a phantom image? Was it magical? What did it want with me? All of these questions flooded my mind at once; and my head started to swim with the impression that I was seeing something quite out of place and surreal.

It did not move when I rapped on the glass. So I walked outside on the porch to investigate. Indeed, the huge butterfly was there. It was a three-dimensional being. I thought I noticed its wings twitch a little, as though to steady its balance. I reached out to it. The creature allowed me to grab it. Each wing must have been between a foot and two feet wide! It was just as beautiful and serene as it was enormous in size. It let me hold its wings in my hands. I put a hand gently on each of its two mammoth wings. Carefully, I moved it away from the window. I released it; and it fluttered away.

I went inside and walked around the room several times, trying to make sense of this scene. But I was compelled to look out the window again. The mammoth butterfly had landed on the outside doorknob to my back door. I was dumbstruck at this point. Did it want to come indoors, or what? I had never seen anything like this before.

The journalist in me urged me to run upstairs for my camera. I wondered whether it was too dark for a photograph and whether a flash on the camera would upset this magnificent creature. I searched for the flash anyway.

When I returned to the back door, however, my butterfly was gone.

For days after that, I scoured library reference books to try to determine what kind of butterfly it might have been. First, I thought that it was a monarch butterfly, because of its colors. I quickly learned that a monarch was big, but not nearly as large as my mysterious visitor. In fact, I was unable to find anything that was nearly as large as the giant butterfly on my back porch that night. Nothing even came close to resembling it. So I took a trip to the famous Field Museum in Chicago to sort through their vast collection and records. In desperation, I looked at their exhibits of giant moths. There was nothing that large with those markings. Nothing was even close. I was dumbfounded.

But the beautiful, giant butterfly wasn't the only transitional figure from my dream world to my everyday world. Soon I was finding bird feathers strategically positioned in front of my path when I would start to get into my car or open a door somewhere. Native people who practice folk religion sometimes refer to such things as omens or gifts of the spirit.

Soon it seemed that many things from my dreams in Selina's enchanted forest were appearing in my physical world. It was almost as though my guide wanted to assure me that everything I had seen in the dream world really existed and that the dream world was as real as my physical world.

Or was there more to it? Was my guide trying to tell me that the enchanted forest related to my physical world and the physical world of nature? Was the dream world a teaching model for the physical world? I still had so many questions, but always found it difficult to remember them once I entered Selina's enchanted forest.

I was determined to take the initiative in my next dream encounter with my guide. I wanted her to take me to exotic realms and other worlds beyond the enchanted forest. So I programmed myself with a post-hypnotic suggestion and held this intention in my mind as I left my body to join her the next night. I was singularly focused in my intent to go beyond where we had been. I had read the accounts of mystics from the east and west who had gone to other worlds, the land of the dead, heaven, and realities beyond our normal comprehension. I felt eager to spread my wings of imagination.

I found Selina in the enchanted forest, watching the small woodland creatures that ran among the moss-covered trees. She looked at me almost the instant I popped into the scene, as though she'd been waiting for me. I must have exuded wild ambition and wanderlust, because her normal smile was replaced by a concerned look.

"What?" she asked.

"I want to see more!" I told her. "I want to go beyond this world to other worlds and heaven itself!"

She did not look pleased with me.

I took her hand and started to ascend skyward with her. She looked strangely at me, as we cleared the treetops, as though she doubted I knew where I was going. Oddly, the sky above the faintly glowing forest grew dark, as we quickly entered what seemed to me to be the outer atmosphere far above the earth's surface. We were quietly and quickly zooming past heavenly bodies on all sides of us.

Still my guide did not pull me one way or the other. She simply drifted through the dark void with me, as though she hoped I knew where I was going and what I was doing.

Suddenly, I found myself standing in a beautiful city, glittering with gems and metals. Selina was still at my side, but standing half a step behind me. She looked ill at ease.

We were not alone! For the first time in these out-of-body encounters with my guide, I saw other people. They were human-like in appearance, but radiant and somehow grander than any humans I had ever seen. Many were walking behind carts. Others were working on a road, which glittered as though made of gold or some other precious metal. Some fluttered around like insects with wings. Everyone here looked busy and quite preoccupied—too absorbed in some noble mission or duty to pay any attention to us whatsoever. In fact, they quite overlooked us.

I began to walk around and noted that there was no apparent ceiling to this immense open area. Everywhere I looked to the sides appeared hazy. Yet the area was very brightly lit, as though pulsing with an inner light. Selina walked a couple steps behind me, as though unfamiliar or uncomfortable with this realm.

The shiny streets of this place were lit on the sides with something that resembled imbedded curb lights. We followed one of these streets, which led into another street that looked absolutely identical to the first. Then the street seemed to glow brighter, assuming a greater magnificence with each step we took. It seemed that we were walking down a river of pulsing light.

And that's just what it was. The street joined with many other streets at a fountain of glittering light. It was a vertical cone or shaft of spectacular light of all intensities and hues. It reminded me of a waterfall, except that it was generated by light and not water. Unlike a waterfall, it made no sound—except for a lovely, humming sound that grew louder the closer we drew to the light shaft. The light glittered wildly, as though flexing great power.

Then I saw what sat at the bottom of the shaft of light. It looked like a man. Only this man—if that's what he was, looked radiant and powerful with a beard that glistened in the light. He sat upon a throne and smile with great confidence and pride.

It looked impossible to reach this man, however, because of a large, square box that stood in my way. The streets of lights intersected at this junction box. I could not see how to walk around, since the box was so large.

Nonetheless, I was determined to meet the confident man with the radiant smile. I tried to walk through the box and started to lift myself over the edge to enter it.

Selina tried to stop me. She pulled my arm back. I ignored her.

I hoisted myself over the edge of the large box and fell inside. I landed in fine sand. I started to stand up and turn to walk toward the man, but fell down. The sand was so fine, that I couldn't maintain my footing. Finally, I got myself hunkered down in the sand to keep my balance better. I started walking toward the man, leaving Selina behind. Obviously, this was no place she wanted to follow me.

When I reached the other side of the gigantic sandbox, I looked up at the radiant man on a throne. Light rained down upon him in a waterfall of light. The light seemed to bounce with energy. I could see flecks inside the light, as though the light was formed by many energy bodies, dancing for joy.

The man looked youthful, despite his beard. He looked at me with disdain, as one would greet an unwelcome bug.

"What do you want here?" he bellowed at me. "What do you seek?"

He towered over me in his elevated throne, bathed in light.

Perhaps I should have heeded Selina and felt reasonably intimidated in front of him. Oddly, I did not. I did not find him awe-inspiring, but rather vain and pompous.

"Sir, I want to proceed to the worlds beyond my own, even to the highest heavens, if I can."

He looked at me with contempt.

"You will address me as Lord! I am the Lord of the universe and the creator of all!"

I looked at him carefully, but did not wince.

"I don't think so," I said quietly. "No, you are not. You are lord of your own domain."

"Insignificant, puny man!" he bellowed. "You should get down on your knees and worship me!"

At this point, I turned to look for Selina. She was nowhere to be found.

"Perhaps you can help me then," I replied. "Otherwise you are just a gatekeeper who blocks my way."

"I am the one and only Lord of the universe," he told me. "There are no worlds beyond my domain!"

Here I got a little cocky. In the nonphysical world, I decided, we have great power with unlimited potential. So I pushed forward, even though my instincts told me to retreat.

"You are a fraud," I told him. "There are untold worlds beyond your little world. You hide these worlds from me. Why do you do this? Get out of my way."

He looked at me and smiled, as though caught in a lie. Or perhaps my answer tickled him. I'll never know for sure. The next thing I saw was my bedroom back on Mount Hood, as I suddenly returned to my body.

The next night, I returned to the city of lights all alone. I gave myself a post-hypnotic suggestion or intention to return there. It was easy to get back. I simply focused on that place. I went directly there, without flying through the atmosphere or without meeting Selina. Apparently, I remembered where it was, having been there before. I simply willed myself to return to that exact spot. I found myself suddenly in the middle of one of those lighted streets. Selina was nowhere to be found.

So this time, I wandered a different direction, away from the converging, bright lights of all the streets. I took a dimly lit trail that led away from the city of eternal lights. Along the way, I saw what might be described as angels engaged in toil. Some pushed carts. Others worked on the road. Other illuminated people were walking the same way that I had selected, away from the busy streets. They looked intent on their journey. I thought that they might be saints or perhaps spiritual travelers.

I walked that way for quite awhile, although time didn't seem to have any significant meaning here. Time seemed more associated with events or when things occurred. That could vary according to one's perception, I felt. How long it took me to reach my destination depended entirely on my perception. Some of these determined souls on the road away from the city of lights seemed fresh, while others looked haggard, as though they had been walking the road much longer. Yet, it was the same road we all traveled at different paces.

The next night, my controlled dreaming returned me to the road again. Some of the familiar travelers there had advanced no farther. I walked until I reached a wooden foot bridge. Some of my fellow travelers stopped when they reached the bridge, as though intimidated. I just continued across the swaying bridge, determined to get as far as I could. I looked over the edge and could not see any kind of bottom below. It was simply dark and void.

When I reached the other side, everything seemed different. Whereas everything in the city of eternal lights had glowed brightly, things nonetheless seemed muddled there in a sort of restrictive way. There was heaviness to everything there. In this new realm, however, there was a sense of clarity and easiness that made clear thought effortless. I experienced a rush of pure thought and eternal truth.

I seemed lighter or less encumbered on this side of the bridge, as though I'd left something behind. Then I realized that I felt no emotions. I only experienced pure thought and truth in this new realm. Gone was my sense of feelings. In fact, the farther I walked in this hilly countryside, the less of me I could sense at all. After a while, I could not even see myself. I was just a soft glow of light.

I saw very few people in this new realm. The rocky trail that I followed seemed to wind along the top of a ravine. I could not tell what the ravine held. My new trail was carved in ancient stone. It sloped down in places and upward in places.

When I came to a high spot along the rocky trail, I found a wooden structure with no walls—only a roof, flooring, and corner posts that held it up. There were a few wooden steps that led to the small structure. It was just an open-air hut with a floor, roof, and corner beams. Inside was a young boy who smiled an all-knowing smile. He looked at me, but said nothing. I passed by his simple hut and nodded to him.

At the very top of the rocky trail, I heard waves of a great ocean or some powerful body of water below. I heard the waves crashing, as though striking shore. I also heard singing or humming of some sort. It was beautiful, but also sad. The singing seemed to correspond to the sound of the waves below me, down the ravine. The beautiful music grew louder, as the waves hit the shore. It would become softer and sadder, as the waves seemed to retreat from the shore.

I wanted to walk down to the shore, but the stone path ended at the top of the hill. The path into the darkness of the deep ravine was a difficult path. I did not know how to proceed any farther. So I stood at the top of the ravine and listened to the beautiful music that was created by the mysterious waves below me. The waves seemed to tell a story about life, death, hope, and despair. It also told a story of lost souls and happy homecomings.

"Are you lost?" it seemed to ask. "Can you find your way back to the shore? All water eventually returns to shore."

I had no emotions at this point, or I might have wept or cried for joy. The song of the dark waters was so beautiful, sad, and yet filled with hope. Still, I could not weep or feel happy. What I experienced was simple, profound truth that is absolute.

Three

Selina's Riddle

I WAS AFRAID that my guide, Selina, was very upset with me. I did not see her for many weeks, despite the continuation of my lucid dreaming out of body. So I continued my soul travel on my own, stumbling around in places that interested me. I experienced emptiness without her and sensed that I needed her guidance and her protection.

Then it occurred to me that the places where I had been without her actually continued the basic theme of her training in the mysteries of nature. The realms beyond the bridge, after all, showed me the ravine and the singing ocean. There was deep truth and significance in all that I had seen on my own; and I finally decided that she might approve.

I realized that the fault in not seeing Selina again was all mine. I was not actually intending to see her or focusing on her when I drifted into controlled dreaming. Maybe she had always been there for me, waiting for me. Maybe she had never left me. Perhaps I had sidestepped her out of some sense of shame or embarrassment. After all, I had brought her to a dangerous realm where she felt uncomfortable and ignored her advice to leave that city of light and its arrogant lord.

My friends at work and around town actually verified that my guide was still watching over me, however. Eyewitness evidence of Selina's presence by my side began to surface everywhere. Maybe this shouldn't have surprised me all that much, after the huge butterfly and bird feathers from my out-of-body adventures in the nonphysical world started appearing in my daily routine.

The first Selina sighting during normal, daylight hours involved two witnesses, whose perception and honesty I trust completely. My friend, Karen, and I were working at the time on a Kirlian camera with experiments in energy photography. My son, James, was with us in the darkroom during this bizarre appearance of Selina.

We had made some exposures and were attempting to develop them in chemical trays. The darkroom during Kirlian exposures is generally blackened without even a dim "safe" light to make things easier for the darkroom crew to work. We had learned, however, that we could switch on the red "safe" light once the sheet film was put into the developing tray, facedown.

This day in the darkroom was a little different, however. I was developing the film with tongs in the developing tray with my back to both Karen and my son, who stood back near the door to the darkroom. They waited quietly for my announcement of the success of the print. Normally, they said nothing, as I sloshed the print through the developer and looked for signs of a latent image forming on the paper. I started to notice that they were nervous about something today, however.

"Who is this lady standing here?" Karen asked me in a little voice.

"What?" I said, beginning to turn around to face her. "What do you mean?"

"Well, there was a woman standing here with us, just watching you."

"There's nobody else here," I said. "I don't know what you're talking about."

"Well, she was a young woman with long, brown hair and thin," Karen answered. "About 5'7" or so. She seemed to know you. She was watching you very intently, studying your every move. She didn't pay us any attention. She just watched you."

I didn't see anyone standing beside Karen and my son. Maybe only Karen could see her, I thought.

"Can you see her here now?" I asked.

"No," Karen said. "She's gone now. She just appeared and then vanished, like she was checking up on you or something."

"Really!" I said.

"You saw her here, didn't you?" Karen asked my son.

"Yeah, it was strange," Jim said. "She just appeared out of nowhere. Then she disappeared."

Not long after that, Selina appeared to another person in my living room. This time, neither Karen nor my son were present, though. The witness was a neighbor who was an herbalist. She had been teaching me and my son how to forage in the woods.

Spotted Dove was working downstairs in the open area that included both my kitchen and adjoining living room. I was standing at the top of the stairs, which was clearly visible from either the edge of the kitchen or the living room.

It had been a very troubling day for me, fraught with danger. A new group on the mountain had been threatening members of our newspaper staff to scare them off a story that would have been very embarrassing to them, perhaps even leading to arrests. One reporter for our newspaper even had his brakes cut before heading down the mountain. Another was pushed around and made to leave, when he attempted an interview. Another had his house spray-painted. In my case, a black limousine with tinted windows was parked in front of my house in the woods and somebody apparently had rifled through drawers inside my house. Consequently, I was very worried that night, since a strange car had been parked outside my house again that afternoon.

I remember standing at the top of the stairs, wondering what to do about all these outside problems. The herbal lady looked up at me and opened her mouth in shock at what she saw. Her eyes glazed over, and she started to point to an area near me.

"What?" I asked her. "What's wrong?"

"Didn't you see it?" she said. "It was a woman standing next to you at the top of the stairs! She was just standing there, looking at you. Then she vanished!"

This sounded familiar.

"What did she look like?" I asked.

"Well, she was bathed in a sort of blue light with little flecks of gold and purple floating above her, like little cubes. She was a young woman with long, brown hair. She was fairly tall and thin."

"Was she looking at me?" I asked.

"Right at you!" my neighbor said. "She looked concerned about you."

I told my neighbor that I had been troubled by things at work and felt particularly vulnerable the past few days. I said that this bizarre vision she had seen must have been my guardian angel. I knew of course, that it was actually Selina. She was still active in my life, even if I did not see her in my dreams every night.

These incidents made me think about Selina a lot during the day, even though my evening out-of-body experiences continued to exclude her. I kept thinking that she was watching over me and examining me. Perhaps she was evaluating me, or simply worried about how I was handling everything that I had absorbed thus far in sleep teaching.

Many times at work on the newspaper, I would imagine that I saw her. Sometimes I would rush up to a woman that I had seen on the street only from the back, and then realize it was not her. These little episodes were always followed by an empty feeling deep inside me, usually in the lower abdominal area. I sincerely wondered whether I would ever see her again in the nonphysical world. Why had she abandoned me? Or was the problem totally with me? I had no definite answers to these questions, only consuming doubt.

Everywhere I looked, I was reminded of her. I could not get her out of my mind. This situation was only confused further by the recent hiring of a classified sales representative named Selina at our main newspaper printing plant. This plant was just down the road from our community newspaper office and served as the main printing hub for three area newspapers. We also shared some resources beyond printing presses, including some staff. One staff member who handled classified advertisements for our paper and two others in our group was this new person, Selina.

It was amazing to me how much our new classified advertising representative resembled my dream guide. The Selina who worked at our newspaper printing plant was in her early twenties with fairly long, brown hair. The hair was even fine and straight, as was the case with the mysterious Selina in my dreams. Selina, who worked at the newspaper, was also slender and approximately 5'7" with dark eyes. It was uncanny how similar they looked.

I would do a double-take every time I walked into the room where our classified advertising representative worked. I almost wanted to avoid her, but she was very friendly in a soft-spoken sort of way. She would look at me with those dark eyes, filled with compassion, and speak in a soft voice that really reminded me of the mystic Selina. When this happened, my mind would start to shut down. I don't know if this was triggering me into a state of heighten consciousness to leave my body or if my analytical brain was just unable to resolve the situation of two Selinas and two separate realities.

One day this confusion with the newspaper's Selina really forced me to deal with the whole idea of two realities that operated simultaneously. Until that day, my dream guide had not appeared to me outside my lucid dreams. Nonetheless, my son, neighbor, and Kirlian camera partner had claimed to see some phantom image of a woman who sounded like my dream guide. I found ways to rationalize these images. She might be looking after me, of course. Yet it didn't seem real, because I had not seen her materialize in an everyday setting with my own two eyes.

That all changed on this day, when I walked into the newspaper printing plant. I remember walking through the classified sales area. I had been trying to avoid this area, since running into the newspaper's Selina always rattled me with her uncanny resemblance to my dream guide. On this day, however, I did see Selina, the classified representative. I greeted her awkwardly and sort of stumbled around a little, as though eager to move along.

Then I turned around quickly, as though to leave. But when I turned around, I saw Selina again! I was momentarily confused. I shook my head and decided that I must have mistaken someone else for our new classified advertising representative. I was embarrassed that I might have actually addressed someone by the wrong name, as well.

So I spun around to apologize to the woman I originally thought was Selina, the classified representative. Only, it was no mistake. The newspaper's Selina was still standing there. I must have looked pretty dumbfounded. Selina looked at me in an odd way and asked me whether anything was wrong.

I turned around again to see who the other Selina was. Nobody was there!

So I turned around yet again. This time the newspaper's Selina laughed a little nervously.

"Is something wrong? You look like you've seen a ghost or something."

"Maybe I have," I said quietly. "Didn't you see another woman standing on the other side of me just now?"

"I didn't notice anyone," she answered. "If there was, she's not there now."

That really disoriented me for awhile. I walked around in a daze, with one part of my waking consciousness in the physical world and another part trying to enter the nonphysical world of heightened consciousness.

What's worse, my desire to leave my physical body would take over at the most inappropriate times. I found myself walking around town in my rounds for the newspaper and leaving my body momentarily in midstride. That can be dangerous in traffic! The main problem is that the physical body continues to stumble forward on automatic pilot with the senses numbed. Consequently, there is little to alert you to sounds, signs, or feelings. I do think that my guardian angel—if I truly had one—was looking after me.

I also found that my focused intent to enter the nonphysical world was so strong that I could now do it without the normal steps I had perfected for meditation. I could simply lie in my bed at night and put myself in the proper state of alert consciousness. Then I would close my eyes and enter the world of dreams.

This wasn't as effective as staying awake, but often resulted in the same sort of adventures in a nonphysical realm of astral travel. The main difference, I think, is that I could not control where I would go and how sharp I would be in random dreams during actual sleep.

Deep inside me, however, my spirit essence now instinctively knew how to enter the nonphysical realities and desired to go there any time it could. I began to feel pulled apart by the basic duality of my spirit essence and physical self and wrestled to find balance.

I disciplined myself to stay grounded throughout the day in my physical body and sharpened my intent to enter the spirit world more carefully at night. In time, I no longer needed to prepare myself with long meditation exercises followed by prompts such as a whack on the lower back or blurring color kaleidoscopes. My body freely surrendered and remembered the steps in rapid succession. I could enter higher consciousness by simply putting myself in a meditative state and focusing my intent. I could fall asleep and find myself where I had intended to go outside my body.

Naturally, I sought Selina for proper guidance. I had roamed too long without her and felt adrift. Finally, we reconnected in my dreams. Selina, as always, was there waiting for me. I would meet her in the enchanted woods of old growth trees and magical light. She continued to show me the mysteries of nature and watched me patiently for reaction.

Did I understand what I had seen? That's what she seemed to always ask me with her eyes. They were soft, patient eyes filled with concern. I felt so inadequate to be her student on these walks. I didn't comprehend the significance of the inner mysteries that she showed me. I was filled with wonder, however, and totally enthusiastic. In fact, was giddy as a toddler who is seeing the world for the first time. Indeed, this was a totally new world for me. It was not the ordinary, physical world. It was not limited by three dimensions. And I was not restricted by my five, normal senses and ordinary human perception. No, this was an entirely new reality and seen with a fresh set of eyes.

Finally, I realized that I would need to sharpen these new eyes and the perception that comes with higher consciousness. Clearly, I found that I could see when out of body, despite having no physical eyes. I could also hear, despite not having physical ears. My astral body looked similar to my physical body, but operated much differently. Consequently, I needed to become accustomed to my new dream body.

Experience in this state taught me that I had my emotional body in the astral worlds, but would even lose my emotions in higher realms. Nonetheless, I had a conscious awareness in all realms. This consciousness became less self-absorbed and more pure the higher I climbed in the worlds beyond our physical universe.

So I began to sharpen this awareness and see without my physical eyes. This proved better than physical optics with practice, because I could experience things more fully with awareness, rather than simply taking quick note of images that appeared in front of me.

I began to realize that the way we normally see our world in the physical state is very sketchy. Our eyes take snapshots of the great adventure that is our life like keepsake memories of a big holiday outing. Only we don't record everything, because we miss so much around us. We size up instances in the big "now" that surrounds us to consider whether they are worthy of a picture. Then we frame them and snap the image with our eyes, much like a tourist who operates a camera. It's all so mechanical and selective. We miss so much. And we never fully experience what we see. If we observe a tree, we might gaze at it lovingly. But do we really experience the tree? Do we experience the rare birds that call out to us with their coded messages? Do we understand any of it? Or are we simply tourists wandering through a fascinating trip?

Selina began to show me things in the shadow world of nonphysical reality that were beyond my frame of reference. Before, she had showed me trees that resembled physical trees and also birds that resembled physical birds in the everyday world that I knew from experience. But then I began to notice new things that were beyond my comprehension.

Like the mysterious butterfly, these shadow images began to surface in my physical world, as well. It seemed that the reality (or my consciousness of the new reality) needed to be validated by my total being, including my ability to see it with my physical eyes and rational mind. I believe that Selina put them squarely in front of me during my waking days of ordinary reality, so that I would need to admit that they did exist and were not simply phantoms of my imagination.

The first supernatural being of this sort that I encountered was a dog with glowing eyes. He looked like a sort of pug and walked with great confidence and daring. In fact, he looked menacing to me. In the enchanted forest of my dream world, however, I walked right by him, accepting him as a natural part of the landscape.

Then I took a walk in the dark before bed the next night. I walked down a paved road that used to be part of the old Barlow Trail of the Oregon pioneers. It wound through woods and dipped into a sort of hollow. It was a long walk; and I felt very centered and relaxed in the cool, night air. It was a quiet stretch of road at that time of night, without kids or cars.

I turned around to return home after a half mile of walking, and noticed low lights that glowed near the ground several hundred yards away. This was the area that I had just covered in my walk. It couldn't be a car, I reasoned, since it was silent. I started to rationalize that the small, orange lights could be road markers on one of those sawhorses which highway crews position near road obstructions. Then I realized that I had not observed any such highway markers minutes earlier when I passed that stretch of dark, quiet road. Also, I remembered that highway markers blinked on and off, whereas this light on the road seemed to glow constantly without interruption.

As I slowly approached the glowing light, however, I did see a sawhorse road marker. And, yes, it did have blinking lights on it. Still, something didn't feel quite right here. The lights that I had seen earlier were orange, while this road marker's lights were more yellow. Also, the lights I'd noticed earlier were not blinking like this road marker.

As I passed the blinking sawhorse, I stared at it. It was almost blinding to stare at the flashing, bright lights with my eyes already adjusted to night vision. I took my eyes off the flashing light and looked ahead at the dark road.

There I saw it. It was a pug dog walking toward me. It was a shadow form with glowing, orange eyes. It waddled forward without seeming to notice me. How startling! Attempting to show no fear, I continued to walk forward in the direction of the oncoming dog. When we came together on the road, I looked away for just a moment. Then I looked at the dog again. It had vanished!

It occurred to me later that this quiet, restful walk in the dark had put me halfway into a state of heightened consciousness. In a sense, then, I had been halfway in the physical world and halfway in the nonphysical world. Consequently, my awareness blurred impressions from the ordinary world and the nonordinary world. My realities were becoming somewhat superimposed, as I flitted into higher consciousness and out of it. Still, the dog had been on that road where I walked. Maybe it still is.

Another time on that same stretch of road, I was taking a walk and saw the shadow of something that looked like a man. He seemed familiar to me, yet seemed to be only a shadow of a man. He was walking toward me in the dark. He was nearly to the bottom of the hill. I was descending to the bottom from the rise on the other side. In short, we were destined to meet in the gully between us.

As we got closer in the still, night air, I naturally expected to distinguish his clothes and face. It was a half moon and not completely dark, as woods can sometimes be at night. Despite the moonlight and proximity, I could not see any facial features or distinguishing attire. The closer he drew, he still looked like a black silhouette in motion. His gait was deliberate, but not hurried. He did not appear to notice me whatsoever.

Finally we met in the road, and I turned my head to look directly at him. As I did this, I must admit that I was a little frightened to encounter a dark, mysterious man on this dark road at night. I prepared to greet him politely to defuse any possible danger—real or imagined.

I started to open my mouth to speak, but my mouth remained open during our passing. What I saw shocked me. The man had no face! He was simply a shadow being! All I really saw was a dark silhouette that resembled a man.

We passed on the road without a sound or incident. I felt him on my back, with hairs tingling at the back of my head. This was unearthly! After several paces, I quietly swiveled my head back to see him—careful not to break stride. He had vanished in thin air!

I tried to make some sense of it. The rational mind, of course, is not particularly good at making sense of anything outside its narrow frame of reference. And I had never seen anything quite like this. Or had I?

Then I remembered the mysterious dog with glowing eyes that had walked toward me on this same stretch of road and disappeared. There was a pattern. But the pattern was impossible to rationalize within any normal, physical laws. What I saw was supernatural.

I realized that I had drifted into a state of altered consciousness by walking quietly in the night, similar to my experience in seeing the mysterious dog. My walking meditation had wedged me between two worlds. I was halfway between the physical world of normal consciousness and the surreal world of higher consciousness. At times, I saw the man from the nonordinary world. At times, he did not exist in my physical reality.

Clearly, there was a crack between the two worlds. The shadow man did not seem to relate to the physical world. He seemed to be walking on the same physical road where I walked, but that was probably just an illusion. My rational mind, fighting for normality, probably made me see him walking on the road to fit the landscape and what would seem most logical. But this was beyond logic. This man was beyond the world of logic.

All of this blurring of the two worlds would have upset me greatly at any earlier stage in my life. But deep inside me, I could accept it now. The boundaries to our safe, physical existence in this world are very thin. Once you learn to cross the boundaries and learn to like it, you tend to cross the boundaries very easily and sometimes without warning.

It would be ideal, I suppose, to respect the boundaries for the sake of sanity and safety. But once you begin to explore the mysteries, the boundaries don't seem as fixed and rigid. You sense that a crack does exist between the worlds and you naturally find that crack.

I continued to slip between the crack between the two worlds at work, too. As with the night walks at home where I saw the mysterious man and dog, these slips into other realms generally happened when I was walking quietly by myself. I would find myself walking through town on work errands associated with the newspaper and then find that I had sort of "blanked out," unable to account for the past few minutes. I would start walking at one end of town and then realize that I had walked to the opposite end of town without any real memory of walking that distance. I was slipping between the worlds again. The restful pace of walking and quiet of the situation allowed my conscious spirit to leave my body at will. Obviously, I needed to control this better, or I could walk into an accident one day.

Once at work, I "blanked out" while developing film in the darkroom. I remember filling a developing tank with my film and chemicals, setting a timer, and then sitting on a stool to wait through the developing cycle. It felt so quiet and peaceful in that darkroom. I just released the tensions and thoughts of the day and emptied my mind. I took a deep breath. The next thing I knew, the timer was buzzing. I shook my head and realized that I had blanked out again in the middle of developing film! The film canister was carefully cradled in my hands. My posture was erect. How long had I been gone? It's hard to say, since the world beyond our physical world is timeless. I managed to salvage the film, despite some overdeveloping. Still, this new tendency to slip between the worlds was troubling. I vowed to control my departures into higher consciousness better in the future.

Strangely, I found that my nightly adventures with Selina in the dream world helped to stabilize me. She stressed what was important and challenged me to see the importance of what she showed me in nature. She continued to meet me in the enchanted forest and show me trees, birds, and light falling gently in the woods. Everything had added meaning for her. I struggled to grasp the significance of everything. I could tell that she was growing somewhat impatient with my lack of depth, however. Also, my strong desire to explore worlds beyond the enchanted garden seemed to bother her. It was becoming more apparent that Selina wanted me to grasp a deeper significance in the enchanted nature scenes that she was showing me and wanted me to focus more on that immediate task before assuming additional adventures.

Then one night she stopped me cold with a question that I could not answer. We had been walking in the enchanted forest. Selina would point out various things to me and stop for my reaction. I would simply smile and nod my head, admiring the beauty and wonder in everything I had observed. She would examine me deeply with her head tilted a little, as though expecting much more of a response.

Then she stopped at a fork in the trail. We had never come this far that I could recall. The road split into two different paths. Where the roads forked, a large tree dominated the landscape. It was an old tree with many branches and moss hanging from it. Many birds had made their nests inside the tree. I noticed that the birds were living in the hollow portions of the tree. The tree appeared to be dead, with no leaves. Every now and then, a bird would stick its head out of the hollow in the tree and chirp a song. Then it would fly away.

We watched this scene for some time. Then Selina turned to me rather abruptly.

"Tell me, what is the significance of what you see here?" she asked me. It was a question that she had asked me before. It must be important, I realized.

I looked at the tree again and saw another bird leaving the hollow in the tree.

"Well, it's beautiful," I said. "I mean, the whole thing is beautiful."

She looked very disappointed at my response.

"This is a riddle that I want you to answer," she said. "I cannot see you again, if you cannot answer the riddle."

I looked at her in disbelief. Then she vanished in front of me. I awoke from my dream with a start. I paced the house restlessly the rest of that night.

Not long after that, I did prepare an answer for Selina. I was determined to deliver that answer. So I met Selina in the forest. As soon as I entered this higher state of consciousness, I was standing next to Selina in front of that massive, decaying tree.

"Well?" she asked.

"Yes," I said. "The answer is that there is a good side to everything. Someone might look at that tree and think of only death. That's a negative outlook. But the tree houses life. The birds live in this tree." I smiled at her, pleased to have an answer.

Her concerned expression did not change, however. I could see that my answer was inadequate.

"I can try again, can't I?" I asked her. "Do I get three guesses or what?"

"You can always try again," Selina told me.

I did try again. I really put a lot of thought into it, although my thought was conducted during the day in my analytical mind. Perhaps I should have engaged my higher mind.

During my next opportunity to answer Selina's riddle, I felt a new surge of confidence. I had reasoned a deeper meaning to what I had seen in the tree.

"Out of death comes life," I told her. "The tree appears to be dead, yet it houses life. This is the meaning of the riddle. Death houses life. That's not what people would normally think. But this tree demonstrates this principle."

Selina smiled a sad, little smile. I could see that she wanted more of an answer than I had given. I could see that she wanted to encourage me, but was becoming personally discouraged with me. Apparently I was supposed to be making progress, but was showing no signs of progressing on this path. Selina disappeared again, terminating this discussion.

I don't know why I thought that I had only three chances to correctly interpret the significance of the riddle. Maybe I had sensed that Selina wanted her puzzle solved within three attempts. After all, there is only thought—not spoken words, in the realm of higher consciousness. Anything Selina had ever said to me involved thought transfer or thoughts I heard deep inside of me, without auditory sound. Had I read too much into things?

Anyway, I was ready for a third attempt at answering her riddle with all the anticipation of a final chance.

"Life and death are the same," I told her, as we looked at the old tree again. "One is the reflection of the other. We cannot have life without death."

She looked at me for a long time before responding.

"All of what you have said is true," she said. "Yet you have not grasped the total meaning here."

I was filled with sadness at disappointing her and also failing. I tried to respond to what she had told me, but was unable to do so. It was as though I feared anything else I might say would be equally inadequate or trite.

She looked at the tree, as though the answer were very obvious. Then she looked back at me.

"I will turn you over to my master," she said. "He is a great teacher."

I tried to protest, but she would have none of it. She vanished in front of me.

I racked my little brain in the days ahead, trying to come up with a better answer to her riddle. I was reluctant to attempt seeing Selina until I was ready. At last, I entered conscious meditation on the fourth day with the conscious intent to find her.

To my surprise, I appeared in front of Selina in a place I had never visited before. She was standing next to an older man.

"This is my teacher," she told me. "He is a master. He will teach you now."

And then she disappeared.

I looked at the old man. He was a jovial fellow with twinkling eyes. He was too short to look impressive in a physical sense. I would guess that he stood only about 5'5" tall with a wide girth that made him almost as wide as tall. He had very little hair on his head and no facial hair on his flush, round cheeks. He wore a simple, white tunic and sandals. His complexion was sort of olive, with a tanned, white skin. His sparse hair was curly and dark.

The most impressive things about him were his radiant enthusiasm and hawk-like attention to everything around him. And he smiled broadly, as though everything around him was both wonderful and amusing.

So this was the master. What would he teach me?

"What would you like to know?" he asked me, as though he'd read my inner thoughts perfectly.

I looked around at an exotic coastal scene that I had never seen before. We stood on the beach. There were ancient sailing ships in the harbor just below us. The sea looked like the most beautiful water I had ever seen. I still couldn't distinguish colors outside my body, but judged the shade of the water to be soft blue or even blue-green. I saw people walking along the shoreline, all dressed in simple tunics. I began to feel that I had stepped back in time. Perhaps it was his time, this ancient master.

"Where *are* we now?" I asked him.

He laughed a deep, belly laugh and put one hand on my shoulder. Then he disappeared. Everything vanished.

I awoke with a start and began to pace my room back home. Where had I been? It looked like ancient Greece. My dream master looked Greek.

Four

Learning to Perceive Color

I COULDN'T WAIT to see the dream master again. So I put myself into a state of heightened consciousness with the intent to leave my body and see him the very next night. I was extremely nervous and excited in preparing for another out-of-body dream adventure that might involve this mysterious man. For the first time in a long while I became concerned that I wouldn't be able to empty my lower mind and escape into the nonphysical world. I followed my proven procedures to the letter just to make certain that I would succeed. I even reverted to using the kaleidoscope color exercise and putting a little pressure on the lower part of my back to shock me outside my physical body. It all worked perfectly. Everything faded to black, as I felt my higher consciousness beginning to leave my body there in my bedroom.

In a flash, I found myself standing on a beach with a beautiful harbor in front of me. I turned around to see my surroundings. Behind me was a cliff near the beach. I could see a rough road that wound its way up the steep embankment farther down the beach. People were working on boats—mostly ancient sailing vessels. Nobody seemed to notice me at all. They were all dressed in simple tunics. Many of the men sported beards and long hair.

I saw a man walking toward me. He had just descended the winding road down the embankment. He was dressed in a light-colored tunic and was short in stature. Then I realized that it was the dream master, Selina's teacher.

Despite the distance between us, he seemed to reach me in no time at all. It's almost as though my sudden consciousness of his presence drew us nearer. Simply thinking about speaking with him seemed to put me in front of him.

He smiled as me broadly, as though supremely happy to see me. And yet he didn't know me. We were strangers, really. It occurred to me that this mysterious, little man took great delight at whatever came his way. He had the eyes of a daring adventurer and the charm of an entertainer. But what could he teach me?

"What would you like to know?" he asked me.

I started to ask him about our location again. He just smiled and started to walk, taking my arm. As we walked, he pointed out various points of interest. He showed me shells on the beach, birds skimming the waves, and sailing vessels that were making their way into the harbor. He said nothing, however. He just continued to point at things for my consideration. Sometimes, however, he would shout or laugh, as he pointed out something that he found especially amazing to him.

He seemed perfectly at home in this place, so I naturally assumed that I was seeing the dream master in his natural habitat. I noticed that he wasn't wearing sandals today. In fact, he wasn't wearing anything on his feet. He sloshed through the incoming tide with cheerful abandon. His simple, light tunic would flip up at the bottom, as the waves struck his legs. They were stout legs.

We walked together along the shoreline, with the water above our ankles. The water was warm and gentle. I had never seen salt water this clear. The sand was very fine, too. It would occasionally kick up from the bottom where we walked and swirl around our feet. Then the water became perfectly clear again.

Eventually, our walk along the shore brought us to a big pier. This was a crudely constructed float that extended into finger piers to the sides. On one major side pier, a mercantile business appeared to be thriving with plenty of activity. Men were ferrying there from small landing boats launched from sailing vessels anchored in the harbor. They appeared to be engaged in enthusiastic trade discussions. Other men were loading provisions onto small boats from that pier.

At another extended side pier, a crew was working on a large sailing vessel at a repair dock. One large boat was partially lifted out the water with a crude crane. I could see that workers were cleaning the bottom of the ship. The sailing vessel looked very old to me, as though it were something out of a history book. Even the shape of the sails was dated somehow.

The workers wore darker, more loose-fitting garments than many of the onlookers on shore. They wore a kind of sash of contrasting color around their waists. I could not determine the color, since it all appeared to me as various shades of black and white. Nonetheless, I could see that they wore mismatched clothes that fit them loosely for their work on the boats. I didn't know whether they were the sailors from the ship or ground repair crews that assisted the crew of the ship. I sensed that they might be a combined force, working together quietly in the splendid sun.

This was a magnificent setting, the kind of place where you might like to vacation. People here appeared to revel in the bright sun. The harbor was protected by a jetty, a narrow extension of rocks that jutted to the mouth of the harbor to intercept waves from the open sea. Birds landed on the jetty to short-hop their way to shore or rest while eating fish that they had caught.

I noticed other shops in wooden buildings that were erected on the floats. People were carrying items from one the buildings, as though they had visited a store. Another shop appeared to be serving beverages or food to people on the float.

This was a thriving, little harbor. Yet the people and their settlement looked oddly antiquated to me. It seemed as though I had stepped back in time several hundred years. I turned around in the water where I continued to wade with the dream master. Nobody seemed to notice me there, except the dream master. Everyone quietly worked or played at the harbor, as though locked in their private world. Or was it simply that I was locked outside their world?

I noticed a small cluster of dwellings at the top of the embankment, immediately behind the beach front. The town loomed over the port from a high elevation, although not that far away really. The embankment was almost a vertical ascent from most of the beach, although there was a road at one far end of the beach. The buildings at the top of the hill had a classical look about them. They were very light in color. I am tempted to say that they were white stone buildings for the most part. There were no windows of the type that I was accustomed to seeing. There were openings in the sides of the buildings, but not glass casements. They appeared to be open windows. The buildings appeared to have fairly flat roofs. I detected an open-air aspect to these domiciles. People were sitting inside their houses, so you could see them from a distance. The shutters or doors that would normally enclose someone inside a house were apparently wide open to allow the gentle sea breeze to waft through the buildings and comfort the people inside.

I would have to describe this setting as a perfect summer day on a beach near a harbor town. But what town? And what people? I felt that I was walking around in ancient Greece. Or was this a Phoenician port? The dress, the ships, and buildings all made me think of a much earlier time and place.

Granted, adventures into higher consciousness had taught me that there is no restrictive sense of time or time lines outside the physical body. The way we experience time as a linear progression of events that occur in sequence is an illusion restricted to our three-dimensional, physical world of ordinary reality. The illusion of time as a restriction is not present in nonphysical reality. Nonetheless, I had never experienced being in the "past" to my knowledge. So I felt amazed to be in this place, which I associated with a dead past. Actually, it looked very much alive, eternally alive.

The dream master looked eternally alive, to be sure. He had walked half the length of the beach with me, wading in the water nearly to the sash around his tunic. His faced beamed with an enthusiasm that told me this man was fully alive, despite the age of his costume. I looked into his alert, dancing eyes and saw myself in them. His full, fleshy face was flush with joy at being here with me. He smiled at me and started to laugh. His laugh grew into a rocking, belly laugh that eventually shook his whole body. He put his hands over his belly, as though to stop it. He stopped momentarily, and then started to laugh again.

"What?" I asked him.

"It's you!" he said. "You look so completely baffled. You have no idea why you are here now, do you?"

"I'm thinking," I said. "It will come to me."

"Well?" he said.

"I'm dreaming, aren't I?"

He laughed even harder.

"What do you think?" he said. "Don't you know?" His challenge shook me to the very core of my being. I felt naked.

With that, I snapped back into my physical body in the ordinary world and found myself in my bed at home. Some dream! I got out of bed immediately and began to pace the room. I wanted to recount everything I had seen and heard in this mysterious place by the sea and the man that I knew only as the dream master. I didn't want to forget a single thing that had happened to me that night. I made some sketchy notes.

That next week, I made arrangements with a friend in town to visit a meditation center in Portland. It was a New Age spiritual retreat. I had watched some very inspirational movies there. A man had made it his personal mission to obtain the movies and screen them for a group of interested people on Sunday nights. One of the movies we saw was *The River*. Another was *Brother Sun, Sister Moon*. One of my favorites, however, was *Meetings with Remarkable Men*. The man who screened the movies for us provided us with free herbal tea and carob candies. We would sit around on the floor or on cushions and chairs in this big room, watching the movie.

The beauty of meeting all of those people at the Sunday movies was finding new friends with similar interests. They were interested in meditation, past-life regression, and higher consciousness. Often, they would gather together after movies to participate in group activities. Sometimes, one person would volunteer to lead discussions.

This time, the group leader was guiding us in meditation to leave our bodies. He said that we would go on a guided meditation to a special classroom of higher learning. Many people speak of attending such a place during meditation. This was my first attempt to go there.

There were probably half a dozen people in our little, intimate group. We lay on our backs for the most part. The leader burned incense and played soft, meditation music to induce our altered state of consciousness. He directed us in a soft and comforting voice to let ourselves go and let our spirits soar.

"Leave your bodies," he told us. "You are going to a place of higher learning, a secret place far from this world."

It worked! At least in my case, it worked. Probably it was because I had so much prior experience in out-of-body travel into higher consciousness realms. I had become comfortable slipping out of my body that way. I must confess, however, that I had my doubts that a guide could lead me to any real experience of significance.

I found myself suddenly sitting on the floor in a large room with other people. The room was all very light colored, as though painted in whites from floor to ceiling. The room seemed to be circular. There were many doors at the perimeter to the circular room. All the doors appeared white, also.

The people who joined me were all sitting on the floor cross-legged in a circle. We were situated in the center of the room. Nobody spoke. Nobody looked around or made eye contact. It was as though each person was having a very personal experience, even though we were assembled in a classroom situation.

Many of the people there were not in our guided meditation group. I thought that I recognized one or two from our Sunday movie group, however. It's as though we had joined a class in progress. There was not much happening, however. We just sat there, waiting for something to happen.

Just then, a door opened. A man walked from the door to the center of the group. I noticed that he was wearing something as white as the walls of the room. It was a simple, loose-fitting garment that was somehow familiar to me. He wore no shoes.

The squat, little man sat down in the center of the circle and then turned around. He was facing me directly.

It was my dream master! I was flabbergasted to find him here.

He looked deeply into my eyes. It was as though he could see into my very soul. I confess that this made me uneasy.

"I'm going to tell you something you really need to know," he said. "It's about you. You need to focus on the things that are important to know. You need to gather yourself. You are not focused. You cannot progress, if you are not focused. This is very simple. Focus is simple. Simply focus."

With this, he smiled at me and stood up. He tipped his head, almost like a little bow of reverence. Then he turned to leave. He walked to the door.

I turned to look at the door to watch him leave. I did not see him there. He was already gone.

Instantly, I was back in the movie room in Portland and waking up in my physical body. Our meditation group began to compare notes on our experiences. They were varied.

Some people reported that they had enjoyed a "restful and peaceful" experience, although they did not enter any sort of higher classroom. Others indicated that they had experienced trouble leaving their bodies whatsoever. One other person said that she had experienced visiting a higher classroom. Naturally, we began to compare our experiences.

Like me, she remembered entering an all-white room filled with other people. She said that the room appeared to be six-sided or eight-sided and not circular, however. She said there were many doors at the edges of the room, and that each door was located on a separate wall.

She also noted that a person came out of one of the doors and walked to the center of the room. In her experience, however, that person looked remarkably similar to my dream master. Her teacher also wore a simple white garment, which she described as a robe or tunic. However, she seemed to think that he wore sandals.

She said that the teacher turned to face her and spoke only to her. What the teacher told her, she said, was very personal and meant only for her. I told her that the teacher has turned to me and spoken directly to me.

She told me that was not exactly the way she had experienced the classroom. So it occurred to me that we experience things very personally on an individualized basis. Higher consciousness, as I had been experiencing it, initially is individualized consciousness. My experience in that higher classroom was very similar to that of my movie-going friend, yet it was individualized. I have no doubt that we both received personalized messages and probably at the same time. I could not hear her message; and she could not hear mine. What we shared was one teacher.

After that experience in guided meditation with the group, I decided to try visiting the higher classroom on my own. I reasoned that I would remember how to get there from my earlier visit. Somehow, spirit always remembers the way.

It was even easier than I thought. I could just think about going there and then put myself into a state of heightened consciousness to leave my body. I would do this at night, as I lay myself on my back in bed. I'm certain that it would work just as well any time of the day—this sort of meditation with the intent to leave the body. It's just that I had grown accustomed to doing this in a dream state at night. I would reserve my evenings for adventure and travel into the realms of spirit.

The first time I revisited the higher classroom on my own, I found it exactly as I remembered it. The room was just as white and round with all of the doors at the sides of the room. People like me were gathered in the middle of the room in a sitting position without much interaction. We just sat there, awaiting instruction.

Well, there was one difference. Another student in the circle spoke to me. At least, I believe it was me that he meant to address. He was seated to my immediate left in the circle. Like everyone else there, he sat motionless and quiet, staring at the center of the circle where we expected a teacher to appear.

I thought I heard this man mutter something. I guess it was a thought, since his mouth didn't move and no sound was audible. It was the kind of thing you hear inside your head.

"What?" I asked him.

"I am dreaming this," he said.

"Yes," I responded. "You are."

Then the dream master entered the room. Once again, my perception is that he only faced me and spoke only to me. I am also certain that everyone else in the room had the same personal experience, except that each person's message was probably different and meant for nobody else.

"Focus," the man told me. Then he vanished in front of me. I awoke instantly at this point, and returned to normal consciousness in my physical body.

As a result of my higher classroom experience, I wondered whether there was anything special the master wanted me to focus on. Or did he simply want me to focus my attention as a prerequisite to the teaching he planned to give me. I began to see a parallel between the dream master and my guide, Selina. Both had told me to focus. Apparently they were finding it difficult to teach me. Perhaps I was too scattered in my attention when I entered the dream state. Heightened consciousness was supposed to bring me awareness. Maybe I was supposed to bring a new level of awareness with me.

Selina also occupied my waking thoughts again. I hadn't seen her since she had handed me off to her teacher, the dream master. I wrestled still with her riddle in the hope that I could one day answer it and see Selina again to resume our walks in the enchanted forest. This seemed so unlikely, given the tone of finality in our last meeting. And yet, I just needed the right words—just a few words. Surely, the riddle couldn't be all that hard. Perhaps I was overlooking the obvious. Sometimes we overanalyze these things. We think too much. We intellectualize ourselves into a tight, little box.

I saw a film about the Buddha at the spiritual center in Portland. It struck me how he tried to simplify the great adventure, the spiritual path of evolution. When he finally reached a point of oneness with nature, he found it difficult to teach what he had learned. He sat with his most promising students under a tree and showed them a flower. He examined the flower with them. He plucked petals from the flower and asked them to tell him the significance of what they saw. Staring at the flower in his hand, most of his disciples had nothing to say. Like me, they did not understand the riddle, this mystery of life.

It is truly ironic that we have eyes, yet we do not see. We see so little of what is right in front of us. And what we actually see are simply reflections of something that happens somewhere else, reflections of light bouncing off something else and glancing off our eyes incidentally. I began to feel that I needed a better way to see. How would I find it? Would the dream mentor help me find it?

My personal adventures into higher consciousness continued without guidance or direction. I had no focus to speak with the master. I could not answer Selina's riddle in order to continue with her. I felt dead-ended. So I continued alone.

I remember exploring and discovering a lower astral realm that was really frightening. Everything there was very dense and heavy. It was hard to move. There were boulders everywhere. The inhabitants of this realm—at least the one I saw, were hideous beasts. Everything had a dark pallor about it within this realm. The atmosphere was clouded with a dirty mist. I couldn't wait to leave. Unfortunately, it was very hard to move in this realm. So I wandered from boulder to boulder, hiding from the hideous beasts for some time. Then I simply thought about returning back to my physical body at home. And in a flash, I found myself safely back at home.

The place I really wanted to visit again was that splendid beach where I had first met the dream master. I longed to wade in the water and watch the sailors with their strange, antiquated sailing vessels. I found that I missed being there, even if I did not interact and nobody seemed to notice me. It was an idyllic setting, a place that seemed so very comfortable for me. I did not know why. I only knew that I wanted to be there again.

The very next opportunity I had, I positioned myself to leave my body in heightened consciousness and visit the dream master by the sea again. I was not disappointed. As soon as I left my body, I found myself standing in front of the master by the shore in that familiar port. He gave me a funny look, as though he'd been expecting me for a long while. It was a look of anticipation. He was ready to resume exactly where we had left off.

"I am focused now," I told him. "I am ready."

He started to laugh. Then he stopped himself abruptly. He mocked a serious look.

"Really!" he said. "That would be good."

He took my arm; and we walked down to the water. He waded into the water and started walking along the shoreline in ankle-deep water. I could tell that he was very comfortable in these surroundings. He seemed to belong here. This must be his home.

Everything looked pretty much the same in the harbor as the last time I had visited. The sky was just as clear and the water was just as beautiful. Antique sailboats were entering and departing the harbor by clearing the jetty that extended like a rocky finger from the shore to the edge of the harbor. This time, however, I noticed more people on shore. In fact, many people were sitting on the shore, watching the boats.

I noticed for the first time that there was a grassy patch between the sandy beach and the rocky cliff. Since I had not explored that area before, I was eager to walk there. I hurried out of the water and dashed to the grassy area with the dream master in tow. He seemed willing to escort me anywhere. He stood beside me, as though awaiting some cue.

Sitting there on the grass and watching the ancient sailing vessels struck a cord deep within me. I felt so very comfortable in this place, as though I were home after a long while. But how could that be? I had never seen this place before Selina brought me here to meet her master. Yet there was something special about how I felt in this place. I sat there watching the harbor and admiring the water and sky for hours, it seemed. Of course, there is a timeless aspect outside the physical body in this world of higher consciousness. No words were exchanged with the old man in the tunic beside me. We just sat happily on the grass. I became aware of a gentle sea breeze. It was so wonderful.

It's difficult to say how long I sat there on the beach, but I awoke the next morning in the normal fashion with no memory of returning to my physical body. It is possible that my alarm clock prompted my return to my body. If so, that is the longest time I recall being outside my body in terms of measurable hours. Of course, there is no sense of time outside the body, as we seem to experience it in the physical world.

It was amazing how comfortable I felt in that ancient port. It was almost as though I belonged there. I probably would be there even now, if the alarm in my bedroom had not awakened me and forced me back into my physical body.

The next day, I could think of little else. A part of me was still sitting there on the beach, staring at the sky and waves. Then I realized that focusing worked both ways. I needed to focus in higher consciousness; but I also needed to focus in normal consciousness during the day. Certainly, it helps to keep things in perspective, even when your life is evolving into something new and quite different. So I resolved to maintain a warrior's attention to details of the mundane world to the same degree that I would focus my higher mind's attention in the realms of higher consciousness. In short, that took care of much of my problem with daydreaming and slipping into altered consciousness during the day.

I couldn't help thinking about Selina's riddle, however. But as Selina said, I could always try again in my attempts to identify the hidden significance of a bird flying from a dead tree. It gives one comfort to know that the path to self-discovery and spiritual understanding has no dead-ends, even though there are occasional obstacles in our way. The obstacles only come from our lack of understanding.

My first priority was to return to the ancient harbor and put myself in front of the dream master. I longed to be there. I wanted it so much, that I decided it could become an obsession if I did not discipline my desires. So I vowed not to return there until I could control my desire and not want it so very much. In a few days, the place was beginning to seem more of a land of opportunity than a wondrous place. My emotions were in check. I was ready to return.

When I felt truly focused and without desire as a disciplined seeker on a path of discovery, I began to meditate to return to the ancient port. I left my body with the express intent to put myself in front of the dream master there and ask him pertinent questions. As before, I instantly appeared in front of the little, old man in a tunic.

He was standing beside the rocky embankment far from the water. I noticed that there was a cave behind him. The cave seemed to lead down into the rocky cliffs. The man, however, was not looking at the cave or at the shore. He was looking only at me.

"Are you ready?" he asked me with a smile.

I only heard the words inside my head. I did not see his lips move or hear any words in the normal way a person hears sound.

"Ready," I said. "Let's explore."

"We can do that," he said. "Show me what interests you."

I walked to the water with the dream master following me. He stood by my side, watching my reaction to everything I saw. We waded into the water. I noticed that the master's sandals disappeared when we entered the water. He must have caught my sense of surprise, because he chuckled softly, as we continued to walk in the water. The way the tiny shells swirled in the fine sand under our feet fascinated me. It made me think of those little glass novelty boxes that you shake to stir the fake snow in the water. I stopped to watch the swirling shells and sand below us.

"What?" the dream master asked.

Then it hit me.

"I want to see colors," I told him. "I want to dream in color."

"That's easy. Fill up this bucket," he said, handing me a little metal pail with cute figures on it. It was the sort of play pail that a child might bring to the beach to fill with sand. Even more interesting was the fact the dream master did not have the pail before this moment.

I held the pail by its little, metal handle. I held it close to look at it.

"It's a special bucket," the dream master told me. You can fill it with anything you want. Go ahead. Lower it into the water anywhere. What interests you?"

I looked down at a large bunch of small shells on the bottom. These shells fascinated me. I lowered the pail into the water in one, big swoop, gathering many of the shells I saw. I collected a good amount of the very fine sand, as well. I lifted the pail out of the water.

"Don't look at it now!" the dream master cautioned. "We'll take it up there." He pointed to the cave in the cliffs where I had met him earlier.

I walked carefully out of the water to make certain that I did not spill any of the water, shells, and sand from my magic pail. Of course, a little water did spill; and I started to fret over that. I slowed my pace and held the pail with both hands.

"Don't worry!" the dream master told me with a broad smile. "This is easy."

When we reached the cave entrance, I noticed that there were steps leading down from the beach and into the cave. The dream master motioned me to walk down a few steps. Then he extended one hand to signify that we'd gone far enough.

"Well, let's see what colors you have in there!" he said to me.

"But I can't see colors," I complained.

"What color would you most like to see here?" he asked.

A strange response popped into my head at once.

"Pink!" I said.

"Then *think* pink!" he ordered. "Pour it out." He pointed to the bucket.

I turned the pail upside down on the steps.

"Pink!" I shouted to myself.

Everything that fell out of the magic pail sparkled in shades of pink. Even the sand was a light pink. The shells were a combination of dark pink and soft pink. Even the water glowed with a pink glitter, the sort of glitter that children spread on their faces for fanciful costuming. The contents of this bucket were most amazing to me! I started to coo like a happy, little bird that had just found a special treat.

"You made it pink," the dream master said. "Now, what other colors do you want to see? Just think about them."

I grabbed the magic pail and ran back to the water. I dipped it in the water again and again, shouting out a different color each time. Then I poured out blue, yellow, red, green, and many other colors in succession. I was entranced by the process and absolutely delighted at my discovery.

The dream master put a hand on my shoulder and smiled at me. He reached down with his other hand and took the pail out of my grasp.

"Good," he said. "Now do this *without* the bucket."

I was startled and confused for a moment, but then began to understand. I focused and started to think in color. Everywhere I looked, I saw beautiful color. I swiveled around and around, looking at everything anew. This place was familiar!

Five
Flying Like a Kite

SEEING THE ANCIENT harbor in color really jogged my memory. I had seen this place before. Well, not exactly this spot, which was probably the dream master's home or familiar setting. Nonetheless, I had seen people dressed that way. Also, I had seen that blue-green water that mirrored the fullness of the sky. Even the ancient sailing ships were familiar to me. I had been there long before. In fact, I believe I had lived there.

Long before I started controlled dreaming in a meditative state of heightened consciousness, I had experienced a series of reoccurring dreams. These were vivid and profound dreams of a very personal nature. I dreamed about a previous life in ancient times. Now, I am aware that many people visit therapists to undergo hypnotic regression or guided past-life regression. I did not do that. In fact, I had no personal interest in that sort of thing. It always seemed to me that a person should live in the here and now and not dream about the past or the future in some fanciful way.

But you can't control your dreams, if you simply close your eyes at night and let your unfocused consciousness drift wherever it wants to go. Like a lot of people, I believed at that time in my life that a person's dreams were random images of ideas and situations that played over and over in the mind, like inner thoughts and concerns without any purpose or direction. And that is probably true of most dreams that are not controlled by setting up meditation to leave the body in a state of heightened awareness. So like most people, my early dreams were mostly about events and worries of the day and also inner fears like suddenly appearing naked at work.

But my series of vivid dreams about an ancient life were very different. These were dreams that played like a soap opera. They had a cast of characters who loved, worked, fought, and played. These characters interacted fully in long scenes that spilled over into other scenes. My dreams about these characters would last all night and continue the next night.

I played an interactive role in these detailed scenes. The dreams initially cast me as a young boy who hid with his mother and other mothers and children behind the walls of a city. The city was ancient Troy. These were troubled times for our people. We huddled together behind the walls of the city for what safety we could find together.

What's revealing to me now is that my dreams about living in ancient Troy felt so realistic in every minute detail. I could tell you exactly what my mother's face looked like. I could tell you in great detail how the ancient city looked to me. I could even describe the look of terror and anticipation on the faces of the children and women, as the city walls were threatened by invaders.

Also, I felt a strong personality as a little boy in those dreams. Unlike other dreams I had experienced, I did not merely observe this little boy or watch things unfold around me. I felt that I really was that boy and experienced everything fully, interacting with the other children and women of this ancient, walled city.

These dreams I had of ancient Troy were not out-of-body adventures into an exotic land. They were memories stored deep inside me. I believe that I was playing old film footage of a previous life inside my head. I also had the memory of this ancient time and place in color, whereas I did not dream in color ordinarily. I suppose that's because my memories were previously recorded in color.

In one of my reoccurring dreams of ancient Troy, I recall playing outside the walls of the city. It was truly beautiful there! It was green with foliage and fully alive. I would play on the hillside that overlooked the majestic, blue-green sea. The bluffs were a quiet place of rustic beauty. There were few people there. My feeling is that most people were tucked inside the walled city. I would sit there on the bluffs for hours just watching the ocean below.

Then one day, enemy ships came. That changed everything. From that day, nobody could leave the confines of the city fortress. As much as we wanted to gather fruit outside the city or take our animals to graze, we were unable to leave the safety of the city's walls.

I recall a whole series of scenes inside the city walls. Unlike my time on the bluff, these were not happy times. In these times, I huddled with my mother and the others in fear for our lives. All of the men had left the city, and most of the older boys, as well. We gathered for group support and to listen for sounds of intruders at the gates.

The last day I can recall being inside the city walls was the day my mother and I gathered all of our most prized possessions. Everywhere you looked, women and children were scurrying about the city to gather their clothes, food, cooking items, and cherished things. Panic filled the air.

We brought our items to a common gathering area near the gates at the entrance to the city. Many people huddled there, fearfully listening for sounds outside the gates. Everyone sensed enemy invaders. Everyone waited and listened. There was no other way to hide or no protect ourselves. If the giant gates to the city were forced open, all would be lost. Everything that we were and everything that we had would be lost forever.

There was a sense of hopeless abandon. This would be the end of our people and our way of life. The looks upon the faces of the huddled women and children said it all. They were beyond terror and not attempting to hide. They were simply waiting to die.

The ground where we sat was a dirt floor at the entrance to the city. We braced our backs again an inner wall that was made of something as basic as rocks and mud. We braced ourselves, waiting for the sound of invaders breaking down the gates. I remember staring at giant, wooden doors that sealed our city from the outside world. I wondered how anyone could possibly force these massive doors open.

These are the last things that I remember about my life inside that walled city. I do not believe that I died there, huddled with my mother and the other women and children. Somehow I escaped the city.

I started dreaming about another time shortly after that. I was still a boy in ancient Troy. In this series of vivid dreams, however, I was a young soldier in our depleted army ranks. I could not have been more than twelve or thirteen years old. I wasn't fully grown. In fact, I was not much of a soldier at all.

Because of my young age and size, I was made a trail guard. I was merely a night sentry, stationed on the trail at night to stand watch over the campsite. The real soldiers and others in the company of our army slept in open tents. My job was to guard one of the trails that lead into our army's enclosure.

This was a forested area, overgrown with brush and trees. The trail that I guarded was a narrow path in the dirt, bordered by thickets on the sides. The path was a winding trail through the thickets. Consequently, I could not see anything or anyone that was coming down the trail, until it was directly upon me.

I recall kneeling at the end of this path throughout the night, poised with a bow and arrow. It was very dark and often rainy. Nonetheless, I would remain motionless in a kneeling position throughout the night, poised in the dark and rain. Any approaching enemy surely would have killed me. Our plan, I suppose, was that I could spot intruders in time to call out a warning and perhaps shoot an arrow at the first invaders on the path. It was a suicide assignment in a way. But because I was not a man, I had no real value as a soldier on the battlefield. Consequently, I was better suited to be a night sentry. Children were expendable.

There were rumors that Helen of Troy slept in one of the tents that I guarded. I do not know. Like everything else in army life, a simple foot soldier or boy sentry knows very little. I liked to think that I knew exactly which tent she occupied. I imagined what she looked like inside that tent. It made it easier to kneel in the rain and in the mud, thinking that I protected her. It took this mighty army to guard her during the day, but I guarded her at night.

My last dream about standing guard at night was filled with rain. I was crouched in the mud at the end of a trail where it opened to our encampment. I do not know whether the trail I guarded was the only trail that led to our camp. All I really know is that I squatted on one knee in the mud and rain for hours in the darkness. I held a bow and arrow poised in ready position, pointing it down the darkness of the wooded trail. I did not make a sound, nor did I move. I knelt there in the mud for hours on end, without flinching. Heavy rain gear covered me and weighted me down. This was not the sort of lightweight rain slickers that are available today. It was simply bundles of extra clothing to absorb the rain. I did not have good peripheral vision or hearing because of the heavy bundling that covered me and wrapped around my head. The rain-soaked clothing was growing heavier with each passing hour. I naturally worried about my ability to detect motion and sound on the trail that I guarded. I also worried how slowly I might react in my rain-soaked, heavy clothing.

Then I heard something in the darkness in front of me. I grew nervous, looking for something to explain the sound. Then everything went blank. That is the last thing that I remember about my life as a boy in ancient Troy.

My guess is that there is no more to the story, since that evening marked the end of my life there. That doesn't make me sad, however. My only sadness comes from knowing that I will never be able to play with boyish abandon on that hillside again or watch the beautiful, blue-green sea below the bluff outside our walled city. I cannot visit it even today. The city is long since gone. It was apparently sacked and burned to the ground centuries ago.

So it pleased me greatly to discover that the place where the dream master meets me is a similar port in an age long since past. Is it Troy? Is it Greece? I definitely recognize the sand, the sea, the people, and the ships that I see there. These people resemble folks from my memories as a boy. But the place could be anywhere in the Aegean or even the Mediterranean. These people could be Ionian, Dorian, or Aeolians. It didn't matter. What I loved most about being there with the dream master was sitting on the grass by the edge of the sea and gazing into the majestic, blue-green water. I could do that for hours, just as I did as a boy so long ago.

When I made the connection between my past-life memories and the setting the dream master chose for meeting me, I wanted to quiz him on this. Surely, this was more than coincidence. There must be a reason. And was I really walking into the past every time I met with him?

My opportunity to ask him came very soon. I meditated and put myself into a heightened state of consciousness. I left my body with the intent to visit the dream master in that same port city. I was not disappointed.

He appeared in front of me instantaneously. We were standing on the sandy beach in front of the wooden piers of the now-familiar harbor. As often happens in out-of-body situations with a sudden shift in consciousness, however, I could not remember what I had wanted to ask him so desperately.

So we walk on the beach, as he pointed things out to me. Occasionally, he would turn to me and smile. He was a wise one, this portly man with the balding head and radiant cheeks. And he was so cheerful. But who was he, really?

Then I started to remember my question. I got so excited, that I couldn't form my thoughts clearly at first. The dream master laughed and put a gentle hand on my shoulder.

"What would you like to know?" he asked me.

"Why this place?" I blurted out.

His thick, dark eyebrows raised.

"Oh," he said. "You mean, why are we here now?"

"Yes," I said. "Why are we here now?"

"Selina brought you to me for training. I am a teacher. Ask me whatever you want to know."

"But why here?" I said. "And why now?"

"But this is a place where you are comfortable, yes?" he said.

"Yes," I said. "I like this place very much."

"Yes," he said. "This is your dream. We are meeting inside your dream time."

"Oh, yeah," I said. "This is still a dream, isn't it?"

Then he vanished in front of me. The next thing I saw was the inside of my bedroom, as I returned to my body. Apparently that was the end of this dream.

The next few days I pondered the meaning of the dream master's words. On the surface, he seemed to be telling me that I chose the place. But there were other possible meanings. I considered what "inside your dream time" meant. Could it mean that it was all just a dream of fancy inside my head without real out-of-body travel? Could the key word in the dream master's statement be *time?* If so, were we actually transported back to my time and place many hundreds of years ago? I kept coming back to the same conclusion that consciousness is not a physical state or place. It has no physical boundaries in the ordinary sense and no sense of time. It is outside the three dimensions and our five senses in the physical world of ordinary reality. It is a realm that you reach with consciousness.

Clearly, consciousness can take you anywhere, if you are prepared to go. It seemed reasonable that it would take you somewhere with special meaning to you. That setting would be outside of space and time. The fact that I did not interact with people in this dream setting—even though familiar to me, suggested that I was not really brought back to a physical place and time. At least not in the ordinary sense. It was a place inside my consciousness. The water was real. The hillside was real. My consciousness made them real. This was my reality. But it was not a world where I could interact with people in a normal way. I could not return to my boyhood in the Aegean, but only this version of it.

The only constant in all of this was the dream master, with whom I did interact. Was it his world, too? Or would he meet me in any setting? And what other settings would be appropriate for our learning sessions? Once again, I had so many questions.

One basic question, of course, was whether to delve into my past life in this beautiful, port city. Admittedly, this had great appeal. Perhaps I had some unfinished business left over from this previous life. Perhaps I needed to learn something about this past life. More importantly, there could be something I was supposed to learn about this life that I was unable to learn in my few years as a boy there.

Suddenly, I found myself grappling with the past, a past I knew so little about. Would several more visits to this beautiful port resolve something about a former life and time? Did I need information from that past life for my present life?

Finally, I decided that I was pushing too hard. The lessons of the dream master would come in the proper order. Obsessing over the past was pointless. That boy in Troy was dead. Troy was dead. I could not relive that life or resolve anything that I might have left incomplete or confusing. I could only move forward with personal detachment.

The dream master offered me growth. His profound teachings would not change my past, but could impact my future. The prerequisite that he demanded of me, however, was focus. I could not scatter my thoughts and feelings. I must focus on present matters with my full attention and intent. I determined then and there that I would not squander heightened awareness on concerns of past loves and losses. The opportunity to learn something profound was too great to waste on trivial, personal concerns.

If I were to return to this beautiful Aegean harbor again, it would be because I found it a comfortable and stimulating setting for my meetings with the dream master. The most important thing was my meeting with this great teacher.

What I was beginning to discover, also, was that my body naturally remembered how to enter a lucid dream state on its own, without my needing to meditate to enter a state of heightened consciousness for out-of-body travel. My body seemed to do all of that on its own at times, whenever my spirit or higher self deemed it appropriate to leave. My spirit yearned to be free and explore. My total being willingly surrendered to this spirit.

It is possible, I learned, to simply fall asleep and have lucid, out-of-body dreams that are instructive and profound. The key for me seemed to be entering a state of quiet and clearing my mind as I entered a sleep state. Of course, the experience of having previously entered a state of heightened consciousness for out-of-body travel in sleep-like conditions made it easier. The body remembers how to slip from meditative state to higher consciousness state. Once you reach this state, the spirit that has experienced out-of-body travel naturally wants to leave the body again and seize the opportunity to be free and explore.

Another important feature of sleep that can lead you directly to a higher consciousness dream state is the way the sleeper falls into rapid beta brain-wave pattern. Dream laboratories have documented how rapid eye movement in sleepers leads to dreaming. Dreaming most naturally occurs prior to entering a deep sleep when the sleeper enters delta brain wave rhythm. Dreaming also naturally occurs when the sleeper is leaving a state of deep sleep with its delta brain wave pattern, as the person comes out of sleep and becomes more alert and aware. At that time, the sleeper is still in a heightened state of attention. Similarly, rapid beta brain activity is present in active meditation in which the serious meditator enters a state of heightened consciousness.

This explains my ease in slipping into out-of-body travel in a heightened state of consciousness without really trying during normal sleep. It doesn't explain, however, why my higher mind kept returning me to the Aegean harbor. Apparently, it was a place of comfort and fascination for me. The dream master was not waiting there for me. Of course, I was not programming my dreams with the active intent to meet the dream master. Nor did I have any particular agenda when I returned to the harbor. That also might be explained by my lack of programmed intent. I was simply slipping into lucid dreams out of a desire to be in that particular place. Nonetheless, these were out-of-body, active dreams. This was apparent to me.

Every experience at the harbor was a little different and not just a flashback memory. One day, I watched them put new sails on a boat. They were those old, square sails that you no longer see, except in history books. Another day, I watch children playing in the water, while all of the boats were out to sea. I walked toward the children, but nobody seemed to see me. It was like walking into a movie that I was watching. Try as I would, I was unable to interact with anyone there. The dream master was not there. I could have interacted with him.

One day at the harbor, I decided to explore the road that led up the hillside behind the beach. I walked to the end of the beach and turned left. I noticed that the road was a steep, dirt road. Actually, it was partly sand and partly dirt and stone. Many people made their way on the road, which apparently led to homes above the sea.

After waiting for various children and a man with a skidding cart to pass, I decided to try the road up the hill. It proved to be difficult to ascend, because of the sandy ground and steep incline. Like the others I had watched negotiating the steep path, I soon found it almost impossible to walk there without sliding and slipping. It was hard to keep my balance and even harder to make any headway.

Then it occurred to me that I was approaching this task with the anticipation of physical limitations. In my out-of-body state, however, I was not limited by the laws of physics. Apparently, I had been imitating the people that I had seen slipping on the sandy incline. Realizing that I should not have such physical limitations, I began climbing quickly and surely.

Strangely, I did not reach the top. It seems that the satisfaction of learning to walk freely in an out-of-body state was enough for that dream. My very next dream, however, put me halfway up the hill as a starting point. One dream started exactly where the last dream had stopped. Consequently, it took me a couple of dreams to climb that hill and reach the top.

But it was worth it. The view at the top was splendid. The hill wound its way up the high cliff and led to a flat, green bluff on top. In the near distance, I could see white houses made of earth, all clustered together in a little village. There were also shops, mingled with the houses. People were milling about everywhere in the settlement. I stood there watching with amazement, intensely satisfied that I had found this place on my own. Then my dream ended.

As pleasing as these dream adventures had been, I decided that I needed to focus my future dreams with more intent. I had been randomly dreaming and going wherever my desire led me. Of course, it took me back to a place I loved and missed. What was really missing, however, was my instruction with the dream master. I needed to focus my intent on meeting him. I was missing a grand opportunity to study with him. He had asked me to bring him my questions. It was time that

I did so, even if I were unable to articulate these questions. I needed to put myself in front of him. The questions would come, and so would the answers.

The very next night, I made all arrangements to ensure that I would meet with the dream master again and resume my instruction with him. This began with meditation, followed by lying on my back in bed with the lights on. Just before entering a state of heightened consciousness, I gave myself the order to find the dream master for instruction upon leaving my body that night. After I lay on my back, I closed my eyes part way and began filtering the light in my head, visualizing a rapid kaleidoscope of fluttering colors. First I pictured yellow. When the yellow was solidly established in my mind's eye, I switched my focus to orange. In time, all I could see was a huge field of bright orange light. Then I began to transform the light to red. The red was light red at first, but grew to darker red with greater focus. I closed my eyes and began to run the colors through my mind's eye quickly in a kaleidoscope of revolving colors. I saw yellow, orange, and red in flashing sequence. This tripped something inside me, and everything faded to black. Suddenly, all I could see in my mind's eye was a black void, a soft and inviting field of magical potential.

This visual imagery was followed by a swooshing sensation, as I felt my consciousness separating from my physical body and leaving the room where I lay.

All of a sudden, I was standing in front of the dream master. But what a surprise came with this! We were not standing on the beach or anywhere near the beautiful Aegean harbor. We were standing on the edge of a very rocky cliff, overlooking a deep ravine below us. A settlement of people lay below us, several hundred yards beneath our feet. White cloud wisps mixed with the blue sky near our heads. Where on earth were we?

The dream master smiled at me broadly. He was wearing the same, white tunic with a sash around his waist. He was also wearing the same pair of sandals. Somehow he looked almost out of place in this new setting, however.

At first, I thought that I was looking down into the Grand Canyon of the American West. But no, this was not the Grand Canyon. In fact, it didn't look like anyplace in North America. It didn't look like anyplace on the European continent or the orient, for that matter. I was temporarily baffled.

I kept staring at the imposing canyon and the little settlement below. The height bothered me a little at first; and I backed away from the edge.

At this, the dream master laughed and slapped me on the shoulder playfully. Even the soft jostling made me nervous, as though I might be knocked over the imposing embankment. So the master grabbed me by one arm and pulled me back. He held me against his body, with one arm around my shoulder.

He stood very erect, as though immensely impressed by the breath-taking vista. He resembled a soldier, resolute in the face of a tremendous challenge ahead.

I wondered whether he expected me to climb down this vertical canyon. Maybe now was the ideal time to tell him that I was frightened by heights, especially on the way down. Well, I had done some free climbing as a young person, but nothing resembling this sheer drop-off with no ledges or easy toe-holds. A person would require technical climbing gear and a lot of rope. I had no training in the use of any of that.

So I simply stared at the dream master with a blank look of confusion, mixed with despair. Always enthusiastic and cheerful, the little, round man smiled back at me. He must have been excited, too, because his cheeks were flush.

"We're not going down there, are we?" I finally asked him.

He chuckled.

"Down?" he responded. "No, not down."

He walked to the edge again and looked down at the settlement below.

"What's down there?" I asked.

"You know this place," he told me. "This is your place."

All at once, I had this odd feeling that overwhelmed me. It was like a pulling sensation. His words had opened up something inside me.

"This was my home?" I asked.

"Well, wasn't it?" he answered. "This is your place. That is why we are here."

I started looking around with a fresh approach. Then I looked up into the wispy, white cloud. Then it struck me. This place *did* look very familiar to me. But it was a very old place, so unlike the world today.

People were flying in the air, but not in airplanes or balloons. It was almost a surreal scene, an impossibility. And yet I knew that it was real. It was my reality.

They soared in thermal heat currents over the giant canyon. Their gliding flight resembled the effortless soaring of eagles. And yet they were people. Well, they were not exactly like people that you see walking the streets today. They were an earlier race of people from a time before our written or remembered history. These were the early ones, among the first people to inhabit the earth. Their ways were different from our ways. Their entire way of life was different.

I was beginning to remember. These were very deep memories, primordial records stored in my soul. We lived here eons ago when the earth was very young. Community was something we experienced as a collective of people in a broad, extended family. Each person was responsible for everyone else. Members depended on everyone here.

These people were not human in the way we think of human beings today. They were not physical, as people are today. They were gaseous to a degree and not totally solid. Their gigantic forms shifted with personal emotion and thought. They could be very dense in one instance and then very light in the next instance. At times, they were unstable. They had to focus intensely to maintain stability. Consequently, discipline of thought and action were stressed throughout the collective. There were many rules.

Because they were gaseous, they blended with the elements around them. They could occupy a cave fully or slip into a tiny pocket. These ancients lived for adventure and explored their world extensively. Everyone was interested in personal discovery. That was pretty much everyone's preoccupation.

Things that we consider important today were inconsequential to them. They did not have classroom instruction, as we do today. All people explored on their own. They did not have organized religion that was practiced en masse. People discovered truth on their own. Healing was not something you would pay to get in an organized clinic. People healed themselves by blending more harmoniously with nature.

There were certain taboos, too. Something told me that I had broken one of them and was an outlaw among these easy-going, primitive people. I was not certain that I wanted to remember what that might have been, but I felt a certain uneasy feeling of guilt and loneliness. I felt like an outcast and not welcome in this place.

People were flying in the cloud above us. I could not see them clearly, because of the wispy, white clouds that painted the blue sky. I watched with great fascination. They seemed to be hanging on to giant kites, with their oddly grotesque arms and legs extended along the exterior struts or frames of the kites. The illusion was that they were flying themselves by simply fanning out their bodies.

The settlement below wasn't much of a village in the modern sense. These people lived in the rocks below. Some lived in caverns or indentations in the rock walls. Others lived in shelters made with stones. They were happy adventurers, exploring this rock gorge and the rough terrain that was their home.

Just as it occurred to me that I should be speaking with the dream master, I realized that I was too flabbergasted to formulate a question for him. What could he tell me just now that could top seeing this place? I was speechless. So we just stood there at the edge of the great rock gorge and watched.

My dream ended at this point; I bolted out of bed with the realization of what I had just seen. My first thought when back at home in my physical body was to begin a precise dream journal. Discoveries as starting as this one must be recorded instantly before any details are forgotten.

The next night, I made careful preparations to return to the dream master in the exact location as the night before. Obviously, we had unfinished business there. I couldn't wait to discover what it was. So I meditated and entered heightened consciousness for an out-of-body experience with the intention to see the dream master there. It worked perfectly.

The dream master appeared before me instantly, standing exactly where I had left him the night before on the edge of the cliff. The odd people were still flying like kites in the white, wispy clouds above us.

"How do they fly like that?" I asked.

The dream master smiled.

"They fly like a kite," he said. "I will show you."

Instantly, I found myself flying in the clouds above him. I was clutching the struts of a large kite. Strangely, I had no weight at all. I was just floating in the air. Then I realized how the thermal air currents were holding the kit up.

How strange and frightening to find yourself floating in the sky, clutching a kite for dear life! But I soon learned to guide the direction of the kite. Also, I realized that I was perfectly safe there in the thermal currents. In time, I was barely holding the struts to the kite at all.

"Now try it without the kite!" the dream master yelled to me.

Suddenly I was floating without any kite. The effect was the same. I could hold out my arms and legs and soar in the thermal currents. It was immensely fun!

Then I found myself back on the ground beside the dream master.

"Now I remember," I said. "My crime as a young man was to fly outside the safe zone. I was considered unsafe. But I don't remember what my punishment was."

Six

The Rock Peddler

KEEPING A JOURNAL did not come easily for me. It's probably easier for a woman. At least, that's what I told myself. Sadly, women seem much better at expressing their feelings. I associated keeping a personal journal with recording my feelings. The truth is that I showed reluctance to put down on paper the amazing things that I had witnessed and experienced in my lucid dreams. These were dreams of discovery and personal instruction. The dream master or man I called the master was a special gift of spirit. Was this a personal gift? Could I share it? I wasn't even certain that I could verbalize these matters in the privacy of my home in a journal that I would attempt to maintain. After all, this was bringing the magical world of spirit into the mundane, physical world. Was this proper? I had my doubts.

But the journalist in me wanted to record what I had experienced and observed. So I wrote about my special dreams in the same way that I would report a story for the newspaper. I recorded just the facts without interpretation. These were running accounts of the events and dialogues in my dreams. Actually, they were more like notes in a reporter's notepad. I never imagined preparing these notes for a published story at that time. They were my personal journey into spirit, my own path. It never occurred to me that my personal journey could provide any kind of roadmap for anyone else.

What changed my mind eventually was the evolving concept that the man I called the dream master was a universal archetype that all people could access. Of course, someone else might see him a little differently, based on their own vision and frame of reference. What changed my mind about the dream master being my exclusively personal experience and beyond discussion was dialogue I began having with people with similar dream experiences. They, too, had encountered a dream teacher and received instruction that was more vivid than most dream memories.

If these special dreams were gifts of spirit, then the spirit should be shared. Everyone walks on a personal journey of discovery, a quest for spirit. This is a path we all share. The journalist inside me directed me to share what little information I had. Journalists call this correlation or bringing pertinent information to bear on shared problems we all have. It is a logical function of community.

It is actually more a failing of ego to selfishly squander information that should be shared. Surely anything that I might have witnessed or learned from my conversations with the dream master was received in spite of my knowledge or abilities. Frankly, I felt as dumb as dirt most of the time when I stood in front of the dream master. His kind patience helped me through every encounter.

It made a difference how quickly I recorded the dream events in my journal. If I waited too long, I lost some of the details. That made perfect sense to me as a reporter. If I lost my notes, it was difficult for me to write a complete account of a story.

Nonetheless, it was always amazing to me how well I could remember these special dreams days, weeks, and even months later. That made them very different from ordinary dreams that are not out-of-body adventures. In ordinary dreams where you review events of the past or concerns of the future, it is normally very different to recall anything about a dream, especially when you do not attempt to recount the experience as soon as you awaken. Often a person does not even remember having an ordinary dream, unless it's directly before awakening.

Often in ordinary dream journaling, too, a person attempts to interpret the dream. Certainly, there are many dream dictionaries to help people do this. Here you can look up the symbolic meaning of things, situations, or events in your dream. Admittedly, I did not do any of that. My conversations with the dream master were outside normal reality. They were out-of-body adventures of discovery in the realm of spirit. Consequently, I never attempted to analyze meaning or symbolism for anything I encountered in these controlled dreams. Analysis, I decided, was a function of the lower, analytical mind. My conversations with the dream master were encounters with the higher mind in higher consciousness. That was the way I approached my special dreams—the way mystics approach meditation for out-of-body soul travel.

Starting a sort of dream journal was one thing. Speaking to my closest friends and relatives about these out-of-body adventures was quite another. For the longest time, I was unable to discuss any of my encounters with the dream master. Certainly, these were amazing insights that I had experienced in a state of higher consciousness. They were profound and vividly real. Still, I could not discuss them. People would not understand, I feared. They would believe that I was mad or a little unstable. Such subjects never seem to come up in polite conversation. Or at least, that's what I thought.

Was I ever wrong about that! In time, I found many people with similar experiences. There were some differences, of course. But the basic story was the same. They were having profound dreams in a state of higher consciousness and receiving instruction from a dream mentor. Many of the people seemed to have the experience of the higher classroom in a dream state. Like me, most of them didn't want to talk about it.

The first person to express a common experience really amazed me with her story. She not only had a similar experience in recounting a past life in a lucid dream, but she'd had much the same dream as I had once experienced. In fact, she was able to finish my sentences when I began to tell her my dream. I barely knew this person, so I figured that she would be a safe person to tell my secrets. The fact that I barely knew her made the common ground between us even more astounding. She had almost the same dream that I had experienced. In fact, she had seen me in the dream scene and could describe with remarkable accuracy what I had done in that dream. What's more, her account of the dream was very consistent with my account of it.

This started me thinking that this dream mentor who had been teaching me in these out-of-body experiences was actually a universal archetype and that this sort of higher consciousness instruction was a universal experience. My experiences certainly were not unique, although they were intensely personal and profoundly revealing.

The next experience, of course, had to occur at the great gorge where I had last seen the dream mentor. My mounting enthusiasm had to be restrained, however, since I had learned that people should not desire something so much that they lose their focus. A certain amount of detachments or *desirelessness* was needed to continue on this path of spiritual self-discovery. This was my life in the broadest sense, a life spanning all time and settings. To understand the mysteries of life was my objective. The stakes were simply too high to be giddy.

So I spent a little time recording the events of previous lucid dreams. The journal that I created resembled fragmented notes more than a fluid storyline, as I treated each dream as a separate story. The connection between these separate encounters with the dream mentor did not occur to me until much later. People, after all, are linear thinkers and basically two-dimensional at best. Consequently, I tended to think of the separate events and various time lines at isolated points in succession. I would jump into a dream at various time lines and locations and then return to my home base. The concept of time flowing up and down, sideways, and all through us at once never really occurred to me. Rather, I thought of time as progressing on a line from some point in the past and ending at some point in the future. But time never ends, of course. Our perception of it ends, due to our lack of imagination and narrow thinking.

When I decided that the familiar man who stood with the dream master at the top of the great gorge was someone I could study objectively without giddy self-indulgence, then I was ready to return to the scene. I had toned my anticipation of what might happen next there. Or so I thought.

Meditative preparation put me in the right state of heightened consciousness to leave my body with the intent to return to that place and time with the dream teacher. In a flash, I returned there.

The master looked the same. He wore the same white tunic with the sash in the middle and the ancient sandals. His head was shiny and balding with age. The easygoing smile on his face was filled with the patience and helpful understanding that I needed at this point. Selina had known that I required a patient and understanding mentor with a sense of humor. The dream master was probably her greatest gift to me.

"Ready?" the dream master asked me. He pointed to the gorge below us.

"This is the past," I told him. "What value is there in looking backward?"

He smiled a sly sort of smile and then hugged me on the shoulder.

"This is your place," he reminded me. "You have chosen it."

"Because I lived here once?" I asked.

"What do you think?" he responded. "That's what matters."

"The past is the past," I said in a matter-of-fact way. "It's best to leave it that way. I can't change the past."

He laughed at this. This shook my confidence a little.

"Well," I said, "I guess I have returned here for a reason. There must be something that I'm supposed to learn here."

"Like completing a circle, you mean?" he asked.

Actually, that had never occurred to me before. I had trouble grasping the notion.

"You need to feel with every part of yourself, experiencing everything fully," he told me. "You don't need eyes to see. You don't need your fingers to feel. Go beyond. You are more than these little sensations."

"I think I came here to understand something about this past life that I did not understand before," I said very carefully.

"Do you mean the way that everyone here flies through the air?" he asked.

"That was fun," I said.

"Fun, yes," he said. "Everything is fun if you're fully alive and aware."

"Am I fully alive and aware?" I asked with some hesitation.

"We have some hope," he told me. "There is always hope."

This sounded so much like Selina that I wanted to cry.

"Hey!" he chided. "What do you really want to know here now?"

"Let me think," I said.

"Do you want to just watch?" he asked.

"I think so," I said.

"You can do that, of course," he said. "You can do that anytime."

Then it hit me.

"I want to go down there," I said, pointing to the rock dwellers in the gorge below us. "I want to see those people."

"Are you sure that you are ready for that?" he asked.

I felt a tightness that held me there in place. I wasn't so sure. Something down there worried me or frightened me—maybe both. My life here had gone wrong. Yet it seemed to be an idyllic life. How could things here have gone wrong for me? I feared that I would experience shame or regret, if I went down to the settlement.

I stood there wondering about this a great deal, unable to decide. Then I found myself back in my bedroom, awake from my dream.

Naturally, I was disappointed. My intent had been to ask a question and avoid self-indulgence. But I had obviously obsessed over some deep-rooted apprehension or fear about knowing too much about that time and place in my life. Life is a long journey with many ups and downs that enable us to learn and grow. There is no need for this emotional baggage, particularly after so long. At least that's what I told myself. I noticed that it was a one-sided conversation, however. Something deep inside me didn't want to go to that place or even discuss it.

After bolstering my resolve, I programmed myself for another visit with the dream teacher in that same place. Part of me must have desperately wanted to return there, because it was easy to reach that spot again—even without color meditation and pressure on my lower back. I just put myself into a meditative state with the intent to go there and see the dream master as soon as I reached heightened consciousness. I left my body effortlessly and found myself in front of the master.

He acted as though I had never left him and continued our conversation immediately.

"So," he said, "are you ready to go down there then?"

"Do I have an option?" I asked.

"We always have options," he responded. "You can go now or go later. But why delay? Don't you want to know?"

His simple logic cut deep to my core and removed all obstructions. I felt that I was now on a path of discovery. I could go slowly along the path, of course. I could even sit and ponder my decision from time to time. Or I could take side trips. But everything I did brought me back to the path. There was no turning back. Delays were pointless.

"Let's go," I said.

He reached for my elbow. Suddenly, we were at the bottom of the great gorge, amid the ancient people who lived there.

They did not seem to notice me or the dream master, either. They continued to scurry about the rocky basin, oblivious to our presence. Curious people they were, if they were even people in the modern sense. They were gigantic in size and almost grotesque in appearance. Yet they flitted across the rocky terrain almost as though they were floating. Some had exaggerated features, such as enlarged heads or hands. They were an odd color, too. They seemed to take on properties of the place where they stood in terms of color and composition. Then I realized that they were only partly physical. They were also gaseous. Had I really been one of them at one time?

What struck me as particularly fascinating about these ancient rock dwellers was their joy of life. They appeared absolutely delighted to pursue whatever struck their fancy. They examined everything that they could find and darted to their next discovery. When they reached it, they would sort of blend with the object and take on some of its color. Some would even contort their forms to merge with the object, whether it was a rock formation or small bush.

Their homes, if you could call them that, appeared to be little more than rock shelters. Nothing was enclosed. No construction looked permanent. These were adventurous souls. How had we ever lost that spirit of discovery?

I toyed with the idea that these were alien people and no ancestors of mine. No, they were not my ancestors exactly. More than that. They were my family. I felt this very strongly with every fiber of my being, as twins must feel when they are separated at birth and then reintroduced years later. I knew this place very well. The longer I stood there, the better I remembered it all.

The shame of it was suddenly overwhelming. These were gentle people, despite their grotesque size and appearance. They were playful and adventurous. In their time, the world was relatively new and certainly undiscovered. The ambition of these ancient people was not to acquire wealth, comfort, food, or luxurious surroundings. They were explorers. Everything was fascinating to them. Their aim was to fully experience everything that they encountered and merge with it. They lived in near perfect harmony with their surroundings, disturbing little.

They had few rules, but the rules they did have were rigid. One rule was that no person was allowed to disturb the safety of the others in the tribe. You could fly as high as you wanted in your personal adventures. You could not fly, however, into the encampment to endanger the others. Young people were certainly taught this rule. Some did not heed it, however.

What I began to remember about my own past life here was my carefree adventures as a young man. My enthusiasm was a wonderful thing and something the others were reluctant to curtail. Instead, they warned me about risk-taking and tried to instill in me a respect for others. But I did not listen. I remember that the others shunned me and excluded me as a dangerous, wild person. My joy here ended on that day when they excluded me. What I remembered most vividly was that one day. They told me that I could not live with them anymore.

The dream master must have sensed my sadness. He put one arm around me and pulled me close.

"Thank you," I told the dream master. "I understand now."

The end of that dream brought me back home to my journal to try to put some shape on this mysterious life in the great gorge. At last, I decided not to try to interpret the events I had experienced. It was enough that I had faced my past and realized what that life had taught me. It was part of a circle that is now complete. Now I could record this experience and move on. There was so much more to learn.

For a while I practiced detachment, trying to purge myself of a strong inner desire to indulge in the personal fascination and amusement of what dreams could bring me. What I discovered, however, is that I could only agree on this attitude on a physical level by analyzing the situation with my lower mind or brain. Controlling my spirit was more difficult. My spirit wanted to be free. It wanted adventure and discovery. It wanted to frolic. And my spirit now knew how to leave all on its own.

So my spirit left on its own one night. I had not programmed a lucid, out-of-body dream. But spirit took care of all that for me. One minute I was lying on my back in bed, expecting just to sleep. The next minute I found myself walking up that steep and sandy incline from the Aegean beach to the settlement at the top of the bluff. Apparently, my spirit wanted to explore this place.

As I slipped in the sand near the top of the hill, it occurred to me that my spirit wanted the challenge of the climb as much as the discovery of what lay ahead. Curious, I thought. Getting there seems to be such an important part of the discovery. Why hadn't spirit simply put me in the center of the settlement, if that's where it was taking me? But maybe the journey is important, too. I didn't question spirit much at this point. It was leading me.

When I reached the top of the hill, I looked down at the harbor below in its entire splendor. Wind filled the square sails of two large ships in the bay. One ship was leaving the pier, just as another was entering the harbor, circling the jetty that extended from the shore as a narrow, protective barrier of rock.

I turned slowly to one side to look at the top of the bluff. It was covered with shrubs and wild ground cover where the rock cliff met the flat ground. Very little of this was visible from the shore below. The shrubs appeared twisted and bent at odd angles, as though conforming to the winds that hit the unprotected bluff. Turning farther to the right, I could see where a dirt road led to a row of buildings in the near distance.

The buildings were white and made of stone. At the end of the road, I saw a man entering the village. The logical course for me was to follow this man into the village.

By the time I reached the entrance to the village, the man I had followed was nowhere in sight. It is possible that he blended into the crowd. Indeed, there was quite a crowd in that little village. People were milling about in the streets. Street vendors hawked their goods everywhere. Houses lined the road on both sides. They were open houses without windows or doors, as we would recognize them today. I could look inside the houses and see people walking around.

None of this looked very familiar to me, nor did it strike any cord within me. This had not been my home, or at least none that I could remember. Nonetheless, it was fascinating to me and drew me deeper. It was easier to identify with these people than others that I had encountered on the beach. These people were dressed in simple tunics of white and brown colors for the most part. They wore a sash around their waists. That was true for most of the men. Some wore more loose-fitting clothing that looked like light robes. Many of the men wore beards and had long hair, unlike the dream master who was bald and clean-shaven with rosy, fat cheeks. The women wore their hair particularly long for the most part. Their hair was very dark.

The women carried large, earthen bowls to their homes, apparently filled with water or some other commodity gathered outside their domiciles in the public places. Others people carried food items away from street vendors. It was a quiet, peaceful village. And nobody here seemed to notice me whatsoever. Consequently, I was able to move about and observe them freely.

Children played in the dirt outside their homes. I could not detect what games they played, only that they tossed something in the dirt and then scrambled to pick it up. They, too, played quietly in the warm sun.

Then I saw the public well. It was a stone structure at the end of the street. People gathered there to speak, even though many carried no containers to hold water. Some leaned against the well, while others sat on the well's ledge or next to the well on the ground. They laughed softly, as though exchanging stories or amusing events of the day.

Something compelled me to continue down the public street in the opposite direction to the well. Many peddlers there were hawking their wares in the open. I walked by many of them, not bothering to see exactly what they were selling. Something else drew me past them.

At last I came to the end of the street where many people were gathered around one vendor. Perhaps this crowd had drawn me there. You could sense great interest in what the street vendor was showing them. Many people peered into his pile of goods for a long while before emerging with great jubilation. Apparently, there were some good finds in this vendor's wares.

I moved closer to get a better look. It was necessary to wait for the crowd around the vendor to thin before I could move as close as I wanted. Whatever was this vendor selling that was so popular? Why did the people take so long to make their selections? I moved through the crowd. Just as I did this, the remaining customers walked away, each carrying something precious in one hand.

A short, stout man in a white, hooded robe was bent over a deep container. The container was filled with beautiful stones of every color and description. The vendor was rearranging his stones after the last customers had left.

Then he looked up to see me standing there. He flipped the hood off his head. It was the dream master himself!

He gave me a sly smile. His eyes twinkled with intrigue and mystery. This disarmed me to the point I was unable to speak to him. He had caught me totally off-guard.

This marked the first time I could recall when I found the dream master by simply wandering freely in one of my less programmed dreams. I had not focused on seeing him or establishing contact in any specific place. Rather, my spirit found him all on its own.

This startled me so much that I could not maintain my presence. I snapped back into my physical body instantaneously and found myself tossing on the bed back at home.

I got up at once and began recording the event as faithfully as I could in my dream journal without any attempt to interpret the event in any way. To be honest, I was completely baffled by the event and unable to explain the event.

The dream, however, left me with a strong urge to return to the village by the sea and the street vendor. Now that I knew that this curious street vendor was my dream mentor, it seemed obvious to me that his container of colored stones held an important lesson for me. Until I returned to that scene, those precious stones remained only a mystery.

So I carefully programmed an out-of-body, lucid dream by meditating, reaching heightened consciousness, and carrying the intent into my dream to return to that village where the dream master was posing as a street vendor.

It worked perfectly. I found myself instantly standing in the street of this Aegean seaport village. The dream master was watching me behind his pile of precious stones. He still wore the hooded robe, with the hood down. He was staring at me, as though I had taken too long to respond.

It was then that I noticed the carefully stacked container of stones that he was displaying in the public street. The precious stones were piled into a container made of slats of wood that appeared to be lashed together. Consequently, you could see some stones on the side of the container, although not very well. Apparently, you would need to look into the container by standing over it to see the stones better.

So I moved closer. The dream master continued to play the part of a street vendor. He motioned to the container, as though beckoning me to take a better look. As I moved next to the container and stood over the stones, the dream master backed up a step to give me some room to study his goods.

The stones were all different colors. There were brilliantly polished, precious stones of all types. The collection was quite dazzling to behold. I wondered why he had not displayed them more publicly, instead of hiding them in this container.

Their beauty drew me to them like a magnet. I started to reach into the container to fondle some of the colored stones.

The dream master put up one hand over the container, as though to stop me.

"What color do you seek?" he asked me.

"Color?" I asked. "But you seem to have precious stones here," I argued. "I see emeralds, rubies, and topaz. Each stone is precious, not just a color."

"So what color do you want here?" he asked again.

"If I could look at the stones, I could examine them more closely," I said. "I could inspect them for defects and inclusions. I could examine their size and special properties."

The dream master put his hand over the container again, this time to block it.

"You really have no idea what you are seeking, do you?" he asked me softly. He had dropped his vendor's tone.

That stopped me cold. I really didn't have any idea what I was doing there. I was just wandering through a dream again, enjoying the sights. Once again, it was painfully obvious that I did not know how to utilize the instructional opportunity of a lucid dream. Here I was out of body with unlimited possibilities. All I wanted to do, however, was play with pretty stones and amuse myself.

What did I really want? Did I want answers? How could I find answers, if I couldn't even ask the right questions? Embarrassment rolled over me. Then I was even more embarrassed for the personal indulgence of the original embarrassment.

"I'm sorry," I told the dream master. "I need to leave you now."

The intent to end the dream and return to my physical body brought me instantly back home with a snap. My sleeping body recoiled at the sudden return.

Trying to record this dream in my journal didn't help. There really wasn't much to tell. The dream master wanted to show me something in his bag of tricks, but I was reluctant to play. All that he had asked me to do was specify a color of precious stone. He had many colorful stones in his collection. Other people in this ancient village had selected stones from his container and left him, carrying their stones in their hands. Why was this so difficult for me?

I realized that I was apprehensive about what I might learn next. It was pointless to worry about what could happen, though, for at least two reasons that occurred to me. First of all, I had no idea what the future could hold, so why fear the unknown out of ignorance? Second, the future was inevitable. So I decided to simply live the moment and not worry about the future. Nothing the dream mentor had ever showed me ever caused me pain of any kind. Everything that he had showed me brought me great joy and illumination.

With this attitude, I returned to the dream master and his container of stones. He was still waiting patiently for me in the street, still disguised as a street vendor.

"I want the green rock," I told him.

"Are you certain?" he asked me.

"Yes, the green stone, please."

He dug deeply into the pile of stones in this container, searching for just the right stone for me. I wondered why he ignored so many brilliant, green stones on top of the pile. Perhaps they were emeralds! But the dream master kept digging. His arms were immersed in the container past his elbows.

At last, he seemed to have found the bottom of the barrel. He stopped digging and settled on a certain stone that his fingers had found somewhere in the pile. It seemed impossible to me that he could have found the right stone without seeing what was buried on the bottom. Yet, he smiled broadly with great satisfaction.

Slowly, he started to withdraw his hands from the deep container. First he pulled out one hand that was empty. He paused before removing the other hand—apparently the hand that held my stone.

"If you really want to know stones," he said, "first you must know the lodestone!"

And then he removed the other hand. It held a very dense rock with a greenish and gray cast to it. He displayed the lodestone in his open hand. Then he extended it to me, so that I could pick up the stone.

The lodestone was very heavy for its size. Bits of other stones clung to it, as though drawn to it magnetically. I weighed it in my hand. It was like no other stone that I had ever seen.

I must have made an odd face at this point, because the dream master gave me a stern look.

"First know the lodestone!" he repeated.

I turned to walk away, the lodestone clutched in one hand. It was so heavy. I wondered how I could learn about a stone that I had never heard about. I put it in my pocket and walked away, wondering where I could study something about the properties of this stone.

I woke up in my bed, still fixated on the lodestone. Of course, I did not have the lodestone when I awoke. The stone the dream master had given me was a magical stone. I knew that.

Seven

The Light in the Cavern

THE "LODESTONE" fascinated me. I had never heard of this stone before and was not even sure how to spell it. Naturally, I searched for information about it, assuming that it did exist in the physical world. Unfortunately, I could find no information. My fascination took me to many libraries, where I spent countless hours combing through old and new books. The dull, green color of the stone that I had been handed by the dream master was nowhere to be found in records available to me.

At last I found one obscure reference in a library. The reference was to *lodestone.* The reference was buried in an antiquated description of electromagnetic force. But the reference gave me no clues about where to put my hands on one, nor the properties or legends of lodestone. Apparently, this was something on the dreamscape that I would never see in the physical world, unless I stumbled upon it. Of course, spirit might find it for me. At least, that's what I hoped.

Later, I found another reference in another old book. This wasn't a library book on physical science, however, but a book on alchemy. Amazingly, Druids and other alchemists had some interest in something called a philosopher's stone, which some ancient scholars said could have been the lodestone. The alchemists were trying to use a heavy, magnetic iron stone to turn base metals into gold. It was unclear whether they were trying to turn lodestone into gold or simply using lodestone in the process. The Druids might have considered lodestone to be the philosopher's stone, but it is unclear today how they might have utilized it in their mysticism. Well, at least I was getting somewhere in my search.

Unfortunately, I couldn't find a lodestone or any modern references to it. So I stopped obsessing about it. That was when spirit took over.

One nice day I decided to visit a bookstore that also carried sideline items such as shirts, incense, jewelry, music, and crystals. By this time, I had abandoned my analytical search for lodestone. Oh, it was tucked deep in my mind, but not in the front where I thought about it most of the time and schemed ways to find it. So my interest in going to this exciting bookstore was just to see all of the interesting things that they carried. Also, I had found a sales flyer that promised 50 percent off the price of crystals. For some reason, I wanted to see the crystal, even though I had a pretty good collection of my own at home.

Well, the bookstore was interesting enough. More than half of the store was dedicated to sideline items other than books. The first thing I noticed when I entered the store was a collection of large crystals and many smaller stones in the far, right corner of the building. Since I had plenty of crystal, I postponed looking there, even though it caught my eye first. Instead, I looked at all of the music, incense, jewelry, and t-shirts. The truth is that I rarely buy these items on a whim in a store, although it is fun to look.

All the time when I was looking at these items, I felt a great urge to look at the crystal. It was hard to understand why I was itching to get over to the crystal. Consequently, I turned down another aisle and started looking at books. I kept thinking about the crystal in the corner, though. At last, I could stand it no more. I simply had to see the crystal. It's as though some sort of magnet were drawing me toward that corner of the room. When I started to walk there, I kicked myself for even thinking about carting home any more quartz.

But as I got near that corner of the room, something drew me to a little spot in the back. I started fumbling through various pieces of crystal like a man driven by a siren of some sort. Really, I couldn't see what I was looking to find. I just felt that I would know it when I saw it.

Then I found it. It was a small, dense rock. It was dull green in color and very heavy. Things were sticking to it, as though the stone had magnetic properties.

It was the lodestone! In fact, it looked identical to the stone that the dream master had given me.

Of course, I was willing to pay any price at all. I rushed to the cashier's counter and handed over the piece of ore.

"Do you know what that is?" the sales clerk asked me.

"Yes!" I said with absolute certainty. "It's lodestone!"

"Well, you can have it, if you know what it is," the sales clerk said.

"You mean for free?" I asked.

"Sure," she said. "It's yours."

This was surely a gift of spirit, I thought. Spirit had found my lodestone. Spirit had given it to me. All of my analytical research had proved pretty worthless. So I just got out of the way and let it come to me.

It was such a dark and heavy stone. It had a greenish, gray cast to it. Really, it felt like no other stone that I had ever held. Why did the dream master think that it was so important for me to know the lodestone? Maybe the stone itself would explain itself to me.

Any kind of iron seemed to cling to it, indicating that it was naturally magnetic. That got me reading about magnetism. What I discovered really fascinated me.

The ancient Greeks were among the first ancient people to discover magnetism as a force in nature. They found strange, rare stones with the power to attract iron. These chunks of iron were lodestone or magnetite. They found that when a piece of iron is stroked with this lodestone, the iron assumes the same ability to attract other pieces of iron. Magnets produced in this fashion become polarized, so that each possesses two ends. These ends are called north-seeking pole and south-seeking pole. Like poles repel each other, while opposite poles attract each other.

Subsequently, it was discovered that a steel needle stroked with a piece of lodestone became magnetic and pointed north-south when suspended freely. The magnetic compass enabled people to explore the entire Earth, which itself is actually a giant magnet.

This eventually led to discovery of electromagnetic fields, which are present everywhere both on the Earth and in space. Electromagnetic fields undergo wave motion, spreading with the speed of light. In fact, light itself is actually an electromagnetic wave. In nature, magnetic fields are produced in the molten core of the Earth, rarefied gas of space, and the glowing heat of sunspots. Such magnetism must be produced by electrical currents; but finding how those currents are produced remains a challenge to this day.

This interested me even more. I started to read about research in magnetism and electromagnetism. The image of the early mystic Mesmer magnetically "charging" a tub of water for medicinal properties intrigued me. Then I discovered that the modern psychic Uri Geller had done much the same thing in magnetically charging a glass of water.

A friend on Mount Hood in Oregon did the same thing for me. She put a crystal into a glass jar filled with water and then let it sit in the sun. She gave me the charged water to drink the next day. It tasted unusually sweet and soft. I felt wonderful after drinking it. Then I started to observe people who wore magnets for health reasons and other people who put magnets in their cars to improve efficiency.

None of this explained why my lodestone from the unusual bookshop was a dull green in color, whereas all of the reference material I could find on lodestone described it as black. Curiously, the stone the dream master had given me was also dull green in cast. Well, maybe it was a matter of perception. I would describe my two stones as very dark gray with a slightly greenish quality.

My own experiments with my new lodestone were not very scientific, I am afraid. Instead, I tried to relate to my stone and sense something from handling it. This is the mystic's way and not the scientist's way, I must admit.

Well, some people carry around crystals all of the time and seem to relate to them. Many people, in fact, claim that crystals help them to focus or even amplify their energy or thoughts. Others claim that crystals can store information, like recording devices. Still others insist that their pet crystals can transform and transmit energy. They wear their crystals around their necks or fashion them into jewelry or wands.

So I tried carrying my piece of lodestone around with me. I tried holding it in my hand. Then I tried carrying it with me everywhere in my pocket. The only thing I can say about the effect of carrying the lodestone with me is that I was very conscious of its presence at all times. Its presence weighed heavily upon me.

Then I tried holding it to my head to see if I felt any reaction. This might have looked a little ridiculous, perhaps, if I had attempted to do this anywhere but in the privacy of my home. Unfortunately, this effort to bond with my lodestone did not reveal any secrets, either.

Next, I gave it to a friend to try holding and carrying around. Maybe I was the problem, I reasoned. I thought that a more receptive person might pick up something that I was missing. This didn't prove successful, either, so I gave the lodestone to another friend who worked as a sensitive healer and psychic with many crystals. This friend gave the lodestone back to me without comment.

Finally, I tried sleeping with the lodestone under my pillow. If my analytical mind could not learn anything about the lodestone, perhaps my subconscious mind could do better. I thought that the lodestone might even improve my health by sleeping with it or maybe impact my dreams in some way. I detected no such personal benefits, however.

What the lodestone has encouraged me to learn is that magnetism is a major force in nature and present everywhere. I have become convinced that the dream master wanted me to learn about magnetism and electromagnetism.

As I result, I have become involved in energy healing work, which recognizes the magnetic energy that is present in our bodies and all living things, as well as universal energy fields that surround us.

Also, magneticism and electromagnetism helped me understand the Kirlian camera that my friend and I operated. This is the same friend who gave me the drink of magnetized water. One day she appeared with a Kirlian camera and suggested that we try to operate it.

Unlike normal image photography based on reflected light, Kirlian photography (or so-called "radiation discharge photography") appears to record electromagnetic field changes of the human body or other living things directly onto film, after stimulation of the subject by high-frequency, high-voltage electricity.

The Kirlian camera process originated in Russian in the 1930s with the work of scientists Semyon and Valentine Kirlian, whose experiments have proved hard to replicate in the West since their disclosure in the book *Psychic Discoveries Behind the Iron Curtain.*

In addition to research by the Kirlians, work by Thelma Moss and Kendal Johnson at UCLA pioneered experiments with a low-frequency Kirlian device to study the energy bursts of biomagnetic healers who practice so-called "energy work" on patients by using their hands.

Our Kirlian camera operates similarly by "sandwiching" a subject between two electrode plates. Normally this would be something like a person's fingertip. Then when an electrical stimulation is applied, a corona discharge seems to take place between the subject and the plates. One explanation is that this discharge is the result of molecules that ionize and form small lighting bolts from the object through the film to the electrode plates.

Generally, there is an almost symmetrical pattern to the energy bursts that are captured on film. The fingertips of biomagnetic healers in the UCLA experiments, however, showed decrease in the halo burst uniformity and size after healing.

My partner and I were interested in this sort of experiment with biomagnetic healers, too. We recruited a couple of women subjects who had been trained in energy healing and worked at a local hospice. What we discovered in subjecting them to electrical stimulation between the camera's electrode plates was that they could direct a flow of energy from their fingertips on command. They could make the bursts flow to the right or the left. They could concentrate the burst or spread it.

Before the dream master had given me the lodestone and got me serious about studying electromagnetism as a mysterious force in nature, I thought about our Kirlian camera only as a device that captured auras or personal energy discharge on film. The lodestone slowly changed everything about the way I looked at life. It began to change how I looked at reality.

One of the famous Kirlian experiments that my partner and I were able to replicate eventually was the mysterious "lost leaf" photograph. To my knowledge, no one else in the West had been successful in this experiment at the time we tried it. The concept of the missing leaf photo is to sever one leaf and then photograph the energy field that surrounds this leaf, as though it still existed intact. What we discovered is that the energy field that surrounds all living things breaks down after a short time has elapsed. Until that time, the phantom image of the severed member is evident in an energy burst that outlines the original physical form.

So I was very grateful for the gift of the lodestone, even though it continued to be a mystery to me. Some mysteries seem to have no end, but only a beginning. The best part of any adventure, though, is the beginning.

Soon it was time for me to resume my lessons with the dream master. I prepared to meet him in the Aegean port again. That is where I seemed to be most comfortable meeting with him. Even my unfocused dreams that did not include the dream master often occurred there. Of course, without any focus or intent in these dreams, very little of consequence actually took place. The important thing, I decided, was to always program my dreams to be out-of-body experiences with the dream master. Sitting alone on the beach in the Aegean was enjoyable, but not very instructive.

That night, I took the normal steps to reach the dream master. I even practiced the kaleidoscope of colors which ends in black. As soon as I saw black, I was instantly transported out of body to the beautiful Aegean port. The dream master was standing right in front of me. He was no longer dressed as the mischievous street vendor with a hooded robe, but attired in his familiar white tunic with waist sash and sandals. His cheeks were rosy with the flush of enthusiasm. His eyes twinkled.

"Well?" he said with a comforting smile. "What would you like to know?

We were standing toward the back of the beach where the rock cliffs began. It was also near the steps where the dream master had instructed me to pour out my bucket of sea water, shells, and sand to visualize color. Naturally, I wondered why we had returned to the steps that lead to caverns under the bluff.

"Let's walk awhile," I said to him.

For some reason, we walked toward the steps. When we reached them, I felt very comfortable. These steps were old friends. I had poured out my confusion here and seen brilliant colors on these steps.

The dream master urged me to continue down the steps and into the cavern. He motioned for me to descend. Yes, this seemed to be where I wanted to go. Without thinking, I followed him. A strange trance-like state overtook me. Something in this cavern interested me very much— or at least this part of me that was drawing me down. Nothing else mattered to me at the moment.

When we reached the bottom of the stairs, we seemed to be inside a very large, enclosed area. Perhaps it was a large chamber. Honestly, I could not tell, because it was so dark down there. But every sound of our feet on the ground seemed to have a strange echo. Also, there was a sort of air current sweeping through the chamber, as though several side passages fed into this large space.

I wondered how to make the space brighter, so we could see better. The dream master must have understood my concern, because he started to chuckle.

"What?" I asked him.

"You are the one who cannot see," he answered.

"Oh, you can see here?" I challenged.

"Of course," he said.

"Then why can't I?" I asked.

"Exactly," he responded.

"What?" I asked.

"Exactly," he repeated. "That is your question."

His words stopped me. It's amazing how quickly he got to the heart of the matter. It frustrated me and frankly made me nervous to enter a dark place. And this was simply because I could not see. Even out-of-body, I seemed to be following a conditioned response to the way a person would behave in a strange, dark place. Certainly, I was not limited by the weakness of my physical eyes in an out-of-body adventure in higher consciousness. Yet I responded in a conditioned way, deciding in advance that I could not see in the darkness. The dream master, in confronting the same dark place, had no such problem. So what was my problem?

"It's dark here," I told the dream master.

"Yes," he agreed.

"I can't see, because it's dark," I said.

"No," he said. "You can't see, because you are unable to see the light."

"But there is no light," I said.

"There is always light," he said. "You just can't see it. Or you are unwilling to see it."

"My eyes are fine," I answered.

He laughed. Of course, I had no physical eyes out of body. It was purely a matter of perception here. I knew that as well as he did, and frankly felt embarrassed by my quick retort.

"You do not see the light," he explained, "and therefore you decide that there is no light. The problem is with you and your inability to see."

"But how can I see light in a dark place," I asked. "If there were light, it would enable me to see."

"You are looking at this all wrong," he said. "You need fresh eyes, different eyes."

As always, the dream master's ability to cut directly to the core of my problem froze me in my tracks. I felt an unwillingness to continue his probe into darkness. I was not ready to go further at this time.

And so I awoke from this lucid dream. As soon as I returned to my body, I bolted out of bed and started writing the sequence of events in this latest dream of darkness in my journal. It seemed important that I record the dream as quickly as possible, so that I did not lose any of the details. More importantly, I wanted to study the dream master's logic. If he were about to unravel my whole way of looking at reality with limited light and remove my darkness, then I wanted to understand the steps in his reasoning.

First, I had to understand his criticism of the way I had always approached darkness. Like a lot of people with a simple orientation to the physical world and our relationship to it, I had fallen into binary decision-making. Everything was either tall or short. Everything was hot or cold. And the opposite of hot was always cold. Is that true reality or simply our modified view of reality?

I thought about the words of Jesus Christ, that great Jewish philosopher, who complained to his weak followers: "You have eyes, yet you do not see." Yes, we do use our physical limitations or believed limitations as excuses for our shortsightedness. Seeing is more than using our physical eyes, however. It is knowing. You can know something even in darkness, if you possess a keen awareness.

Other animals display awareness. They sense things, without analyzing them. Even plants have awareness of a sort. They curve their vines around corners, searching for water and light that is beyond their immediate surroundings. Sometimes, it takes a plant a long while to grow around the corners that will eventually bring them to light. But they make that lifelong commitment, knowing that there is light just around the corner.

This also made me think about the simplistic way that people tend to look at things, foolishly believing that they understand absolute reality. People, however, tend to think in absolute terms that are mutually exclusive. For instance, we think of something that is *up* as *not down* or something that is *short* as *not tall*. Actually, this is just a matter of personal perspective. A small child tends to see even short adults as tall. And a yogi who does a headstand naturally sees what upright people call *up* as *down* from his upside-down position.

An inventor that I had interviewed once for a feature article told me that an inventor looks at everything from a different perspective to gain a fresh approach. He told me to lie on the floor and describe the items on a table above me. Of course, I told him that I could not see them from my vantage point. So he suggested that I get up on one knee at eye level to one side of the table. Of course, I could see only some of the items at an angle. Only when I stood up over the table could I identify every item accurately on the table. He told me that inventors seek a higher vantage point. They do not accept the common description of things and the way things work, because they realize that most of us do not see things from a proper vantage point. In fact, we tend to accept a group consensus definition of reality. In order to think outside of the box—as he called it, a truly inventive thinker needs to gain a fresh perspective.

I didn't write any of this conjecture into my dream journal. Only the events of the dream and conversations with the dream master went into my journal. The reporter in me did not want to embellish the concrete facts, certainly not at this stage. The seeker in me realized that my analytical mind was inadequate to resolve the questions that were raised in a state of higher consciousness. These were questions beyond this world, but with implications that seemed to spill over into the physical world.

Clearly, I needed a fresh perspective that could only be gained by experience in that cavern. I needed the insight of the dream master to guide me. It was time to return to face the darkness and also the light, if I could find it. My worldview of reality was about to be challenged, and I could postpone it no longer.

So I programmed myself to return to that dark cavern and meet with the dream master. I meditated carefully and even used the color kaleidoscope exercise to make certain that I would reach my destination quickly and accurately. When the color wheel faded to black, I felt myself snap out of my body. Then I found myself immediately in the dark cavern, again facing the dream master.

It was difficult to see him at first in the darkness. I told myself that my eyes hadn't adjusted to the darkness, but that couldn't be true. There are no physical eyes out of body. We see with our awareness, or we don't see at all. Nonetheless, I squinted to try to see the dream master better.

He laughed.

"Are you ready to resume?" he asked me.

"Yes," I said. "I realize that there is something here that I need to understand."

He nodded his head and smiled, seemingly pleased.

"You have told me that you think there is no light in this place, correct?" he asked me.

"Yes," I answered. "I see no light in this place."

"And I have told you that there is light here, even though you are unable or unwilling to see it," he added.

"Yes," I said.

"Why do you believe there is no light in this room?"

"Because I cannot see," I repeated.

"No, you said that you cannot see the light," he reminded me.

"Yes, that's true," I admitted.

"What would we need in this space to have light, then?" he asked. "Where would the light come from?"

I could only think of an electric light bulb and a socket hanging from the ceiling. I knew that was the wrong answer for this ancient setting, but was a situation familiar to me. The dream master seemed to read my thought instantly.

"There are no secrets here," he chided me. "If you are thinking about electric lights, tell me."

"Well, yes," I said reluctantly. "If we had an electrical outlet coming down from the ceiling, I suppose we would have light here then."

"Let's test that," he said quickly, raising one hand into the air.

An electric cord lowered out of nowhere and dangled in our faces. It had a socket on one end, but no lamp.

"Here is your electrical service," he said. "Now do you see better?"

"No, of course not," I answered. "There is no bulb in that socket."

"Ah!" he exclaimed in mock surprise. "So electricity would illuminate our space. And yet here's an electrical service cord that does not produce any light at all. Is that what you are saying?"

"Right. It's missing something."

"So there is no electricity service here?" he chided.

"No, there is no electricity here."

"Alright," he said. "You can test your theory. Put your finger into that socket and test if there is no electricity."

"Oh, no!" I protested. "I'll get shocked!"

"Aha!" he exclaimed. "Shocked by electricity?" he asked.

"Yes!" I said. "I can't do that."

"So what you seem to be saying is that there is energy potential here," he said. "You are just unable to tap it correctly or use it to your satisfaction."

"Yes, that's it."

The dream master laughed out loud with a deep belly laugh; and I was reminded of the trickster who had posed as a street vendor. Obviously, he was setting me up. Anxiety overwhelmed me.

"What you are saying," he said slowly, "is that there is unlimited power to generate light that comes out of that service wire. That electricity is a force that could light this room. Yet something is lacking?"

"Yes," I answered. "There is no light bulb."

"And how would the light bulb look? Would you know it, if you saw it?"

"Yes," I said. "It would glow brightly."

"Ah!" he said. "Then we can fix that."

The end of the electrical cord started to glow. This startled me; and I jumped back in surprise.

"Oh, do you want something less bright?" he asked.

The glowing became more subdued.

"No," I said.

"Alright," the dream master said. "We'll make it glow brightly then."

The room was suddenly very bright with the glowing light. Then the light dimmed a little.

"Do you want to try it yourself?" the dream master asked me.

"Try what?" I asked.

"Make the room bright," he said. "Make it glow."

I look at him with a puzzled expression.

"Come on!" he said. "This is easy. You just tap the unlimited potential of the energy in the room and put it to good use. Make the room glow!"

I followed his orders and concentrated on making the room glow brighter. To my amazement, the light did increase. I found that I could make it bright and then darker.

"You're playing now," he chided. "But I believe you are beginning to understand."

The lighter room enabled me to look around and see the cavern for the first time. It was large and barren. There was nothing inside the cavern except the two of us, as far as I could see. The ground was dirt with stones imbedded everywhere. We seemed to be totally enclosed without any exits or passageways. There were some small cracks in the walls, but there did not seem to be any light coming through these walls. The ceiling was light-proof, as well, as best I could tell.

It was amazing to me that I could have seen the dream master at all in this dark cavern. But as the dream master said, the space was never totally dark—just not brightly lit. I suppose that it was largely a matter of perspective.

Certainly the potential to see the room more brightly lit was always present. Energy was at our disposal, if we had imagination and exercised it.

Eight

Seeing Beyond the Walls

IT WAS TEMPTING to add interpretation to this last conversation with the dream master when I recorded the event in my dream journal. What he'd told me in the dark cavern really changed my life forever or at least how I looked at reality. The implications of what he suggested were far-reaching. There were forces in nature that could be tapped. Energy was all around us. I don't believe for a minute that an electrical cord actually hung from the ceiling of that cavern in that ancient port city, at least not before we had entered the cavern. It just wasn't likely to be there in such an ancient time or such an undeveloped cavern. The dangling cord did represent a point of view, however. That point, according to the dream master, was all about potentiality. We have the potential to tap energy. We have the potential to make our world brighter. We can make the room glow.

What it takes is imagination, belief in the unseen forces in nature, and awareness. Ultimately, we must touch the world with our will. This requires focus. It also requires intent.

Certainly this all appears easier to achieve in the dream world in an out-of-body state. In this state of higher consciousness, one is not limited by the physical laws of the universe or the physical limitations of the human body and its many sensory distractions. Also, the higher mind has unlimited potential.

Everything the dream master and Selina had taught me, however, suggested that whatever was demonstrated to me out of body could be manifested in the physical world, as well. The giant butterfly had appeared first in a dream, but then in my physical world. Then the shadow man, dog, and lodestone manifested in my physical world, after first appearing in lucid dreams. Even Selina had appeared in the physical world, seen by several others in addition to me.

So it seemed to me that the instruction of the dream master was intended to impact my view of reality in the physical world, as well. He was expanding my consciousness and certainly broadening my perspective.

Thus far, however, he had been showing me only possibilities and stretching my vision of reality. Until now, he had not suggested any rules. He had always waited for me to determine where to go, what to do, and when to begin. Like any good teacher, he waited for the student to indicate what is needed and when to begin the instruction. He also seemed to read me pretty well. Honestly, I think that he knew me and my needs pretty well, but waited for me to recognize them first. Spirit always knows, of course, if you quietly wait and listen. My spirit seemed to be remembering a lot about where it had been and concerns that it needed to address.

In this last dream in the cavern, the dream master cautioned me not to play with the forces of nature, once I had learned to tap them. I thought this a little odd at first, considering how he had encouraged me to engage them at will.

Eventually, however, I could see the sense in this. He seemed to be saying not to treat them carelessly or manipulate them without good intent. Why cultivate the power to channel unseen forces of nature without having the self-control to utilize them responsibly and not capriciously? My need for light was small. I only needed enough light to see the inside of that cavern for the short time that I was there. I did not need intensely bright light all over the world. Nor does the entire world want intensely bright light in all corners all of the time. Sometimes a baby needs to sleep with the light turned down. Sometimes the flowers need to fold for the evening.

Of course, none of this conjecture appeared in my dream journal. The serious reporter in me demanded that I only record the events of the dream and the conversation with the dream master. Speculation into meaning was something that happened internally with me, as my total being absorbed the shock of these meetings with the dream master. If I tried to interpret my dreams in the normal manner, something deep inside me told me that I might screw it up.

Besides, there was nothing symbolic in anything that the dream master had told me. From what I could tell, he was pretty concrete and straightforward about everything. At least, that's the way it appeared to me. Yes, the electrical cord was a device he used to make a point. But it was pretty obvious that he was talking about accessing the potential power all around us. He used the electrical cord, because that's the example I gave him as a power source for illumination. So he was adapting to my frame of reference to make a point that would be easy for me to understand.

Curiosity about the cavern still consumed me, nevertheless. Why had the dream master taken me down there? Usually, I would select the place. Of course, the cave made the perfect darkroom for his demonstration with the electrical cord. Making the dark confines glow was a pretty spectacular lesson.

But I still wondered how the chambers apparently dead-ended there, with no passageways. Most caverns go deep, with lots of passages. Or at least that was my impression. The truth is that I am a bit claustrophobic and didn't frequent caverns. In fact, that was my first, as far as I can remember.

There were also small cracks in the walls. I wondered about them and whether they were significant. Despite my claustrophobia, the cavern was someplace I definitely wanted to explore. Perhaps the only way to explain this feeling would be to examine the higher mind out of body. Clearly, that part of me did not carry the same psychological baggage.

Emotions seemed to follow me in my out-of-body travel, however. Why not fear? Well, I had experience fear before in my encounters with the dream master. But I also had experience greater ambition and courage in my lucid dreaming with him. Part of the explanation might be my trust in the dream master. Another reason was my sense of adventure out of body. Spirit seeks answers; and answers seem to come through trial and journey. That's probably why it's called discovery. It's a journey of the soul.

Consequently, I resolved to return to that same cavern to meet with the dream master again. I sensed that we had unfinished business there or something I needed to see or know. It struck me as odd that something I needed to see or know would be buried in the bowels of the earth thousands of years ago. This was not exactly a hero's journey in the grand sense, I guess, but a personal one.

I felt that I had a personal appointment with the dream master back in that cavern and programmed myself for a lucid, out-of-body dream that would bring me to that exact spot and time. As soon as my higher consciousness left my body, I found myself standing inside the chamber again with the dream master. Curiously, I could see him better now, although the light was still dim.

He laughed at me in a jovial way and reached out to grab my arm in his familiar fashion.

"Still having trouble with darkness?" he asked.

I looked around the dark chamber and focused my attention on making it glow brighter.

It occurred to me that I needed to project my will. I concentrated on what would be the abdominal region of my astral body. Then I tried to focus my intent to send energy from that region. That seemed to energize my thoughts.

At last, the room was a little brighter, although still dimly lit.

"Charming," I said. "Romantic."

The dream master chuckled.

The slightly brighter room allowed me to look around a little better to inspect the chamber. The mystery of our setting fascinated me. Naturally, I wondered why the dream master had chosen this place in the first place. That curiosity had encouraged me to return for a better examination of the cavern.

I started to walk from one side of the chamber to the other, inspecting the walls for openings. Somehow, I couldn't believe that this chamber was dead-ended.

"Things aren't always as they first appear," the dream master cautioned me.

"I see," I replied.

"Do you really?" he challenged.

Air currents swept through the chamber. Wondering whether they came from the entry that led upstairs to the beach outside, I walked to that corner of the chamber. It was difficult to tell whether the entire breeze came from that direction. Did north wind feel different from south wind? Is all wind the same? I felt like a child playing in a sand lot, hoping to find something out of pure childish luck.

I returned to the far wall and felt the air current there. Was the air simply trapped in the chamber and swirling around? No, it seemed to be coming through the wall itself.

So I tested that theory on another wall. This time I got much closer. The air current here felt a little different. Could that be because it was circulating in a different part of the chamber and bouncing off different walls? That would make perfect sense, if there were only one source for the air current. Somehow these currents all felt a little different to me.

Then I began to question how I could feel or smell anything without my physical body. Was I sensing on a different level out of body? Did my astral body have sensors?

The dream master walked over to me, as I leaned into a far corner of the chamber. He put an arm around me.

"Do not doubt your perception," he said. "Trust your instincts."

"But how can I really feel anything without my sense of touch or my sense of smell?" I asked in a quiet, confused voice.

He heard my thoughts clearly, however.

"You can see without eyes," he reminded me. "Surely you can smell without a nose."

As a reflex, I self-consciously felt where my nose would be.

He laughed.

"We are more than our physical senses," he said. "Much more."

So I tried sniffing the air currents against the wall. That seemed odd, because I couldn't hear the sniffing sounds of an active nose testing the wind.

"And what have you found?" he asked.

"That I can't be sure I'm sniffing, if I can't hear my nose twitch."

He laughed and laughed.

"That isn't funny," I said self-consciously. "Or is it?"

"Sure it is," he said. "You are very funny."

This made me laugh. With more confidence, I circled the room, walking alongside the walls. I felt them carefully and attempted to fully absorb any sense of air current that might be wafting near the walls. The more I did this, the easier it became.

A realization came over me that I could become conscious of the sensation of air current and even the scent of it by integrating myself with the air itself. In a sense, I was becoming one with the air around me and relating to the air around me. Every essence of my being was absorbed in this integration.

In a way, this was better than using my physical senses. If I had felt the air rushing off my skin or smelled the air currents, I would have interpersonalized the experience. I would have become self-absorbed in the experience, relating only to the comfort level I attained internally from the intake of air. The senses would have taken me down a self-indulgent path, by contrast.

My out-of-body higher consciousness comingled with the air in the cavern. In this manner, I not only experienced the air currents. I also became the air currents, experiencing existence as they knew it. Consequently, the experience wasn't solely from my selfish perspective through the titillation of my senses, but a cooperative experience that allowed me to share the perspective of the air itself.

Once I had fully made this shift in my conscious perspective, I had no trouble whatsoever in identifying the air currents, their directional flow, and their origins. What a revelation!

The air currents were coming through cracks in the walls. Moreover, there were cross-currents of air flowing into the chamber from a number of directions. The air was fresh and not stale, as one might expect from dead-end slips and shallow cracks in the wall that seemed to lead nowhere.

But that made no sense to me. The air had to come from an outside source, I reasoned. Did deep cracks and crevices in the cavern lead all the way up to the open air at the top? Or was the air recirculated? No, recirculated air would not be this fresh, I decided.

Perhaps my closeness to the air itself could tell me more about this. I focused on the air, feeling it rush through me. All I could sense from it, however, was that it came from outside the chamber. It came swirling into the chamber with the sense that it had slipped through a narrow opening and then enjoyed the expansiveness of filling the relative vacuum of the inner chamber.

It was slowly dawning on my consciousness that the air currents were hinting at something quite important here. If they had slipped through openings from the other side of the inner chamber, then some other chambers existed on the other side of these walls. Why hadn't I seen this before? Was it because I had been unable to see light coming through the tiny cracks in the walls? Seeing no light that filtered into my space, I assumed that no other space could exist beyond my confining walls.

Aha! At last I felt that moment of sudden realization. My perspective had been defined solely by what I could see; yet I had already learned that I did not see all that well. There was more to all of this than I had first thought. Isn't that always the way it is with us?

When the fog cleared on my self-induced confusion, I felt this wonderful sense of comfort and inner peace. At last, I was no longer at odds with my surroundings. The confines of the cavern no longer troubled me.

Apparently my spirit felt satisfied with the events of this encounter, because I suddenly felt my consciousness returning to my physical body back in my bedroom at home. I snapped back into my body so abruptly that I bolted out of bed.

I rushed to my dream journal to record the events of this last dream in as much detail as possible, so that I would recall everything accurately, particularly my conversation with the dream master.

Lately I had gone to the safe approach of quickly outlining the events of the dream, so that I didn't forget anything once I returned to the many distractions of the physical world. That enabled me to capture the essence of the dream and then expand on the outline form.

This seemed to work. I found that even a couple of words would save something in my memory. Of course, the very exercise of recording key elements of the dream in the journal immediately after the experience seemed to make it easier to remember the complete dream later.

In jotting down the events of the dream, however, I realized that something was still unresolved there in that cavern. What was on the other side of the walls to that inner chamber? The air currents clearly demonstrated to me that fresh air was eking through cracks in the walls from other chambers or passages on the other side. It was difficult to see anything through these narrow slits in the walls, but the air currents proved to my satisfaction that another place existed on the other side.

Strangely, this made me think about my cats. It's commonly believed that cats aren't abstract thinkers that are capable of picturing something or someone on another side of a wall. Since this other creature or thing exists outside of the cat's immediate sphere of reference and the narrow confines of its reality, it doesn't register with the cat whatsoever.

That's the commonly held viewpoint of people who observe cats. My own observation of cats admittedly has been limited to cats that I have known and particularly my own house cats. My cats don't have this problem of locational identification, as people sometimes describe it.

In fact, my largest tomcat enjoys hiding behind doors when he senses another cat on the other side. Sometimes the door is cracked slightly ajar. Sometimes the door is closed. Other times, the door is the opaque cat door that allows small felines to enter the house through a tiny, hinged opening. Even though my tomcat can't see another cat on the other side of the door, he perks to attention the instant he senses another cat on the opposite side of a door. Then he waits patiently for his potential victim to come through the door, so he can pounce playfully. It's a game to him; and he's good at it. He can wait a long time for someone to open the door for a cat he senses on the other side of a closed door or for the cat to wander through a cracked door on its own. His attention is focused on his target on the other side.

So maybe cats are better abstract thinkers than we are. At least, I could make the case that my top cat is better at bilocational identification than I am. Certainly, it would appear than he has a broader sense of reality than my limited focus of what I can immediately see in front of me.

Now, I suppose that a veterinarian or animal behaviorist might argue with me at giving my cat so much credit. They might argue, in fact, that a cat lacks the physical attributes necessary to do what I have described. I would counter, however, that this is not an isolated incident. Admittedly, I have not shared my life with a lot of cats. Of the few cats I have known, though, at least two others had the same awareness as my big tomcat who could visualize what lies behind walls.

A wild kitten that lived in our farmhouse when I was a boy decided to crawl into the rafters of our house one day. The only problem was that it didn't come out for dinner that night. Naturally, we were all concerned at my house. My father looked into the rafters and told me some sad news. He noted that the rafters in our attic ran like a maze with lots of dead ends. It would be very difficult, he said, for the little kitten to find its way out of the maze.

The kitten remained lost in the maze in our rafters for another day. Then I thought of a plan. The only thing that I could think to do was knock on one of the boards at the edge of the rafters. The board that I selected was the end board of one of those dead-end passageways. The kitten might hear the knocking, I thought, and dead-reckon its away around the maze in the direction of the knocking. So I sat there in the closet, knocking on a board in hopes that this little kitten could determine how to negotiate the maze and return to me.

I did this for approximately ten minutes. Suddenly, the little kitten emerged from the maze. Of course, the howling feline was dehydrated and hungry. But it was also pretty proud of itself to find its way back by following my beacon. Pilots who negotiate their way through fog with dead-reckoning have it easier than that little cat, which had to go through a labyrinth.

Years later, I had an angry and possessive cat named Mildred who hopped out of a crack in my car's window after a disagreement. She didn't want to ride in the car. I was taking her to my new home in Oregon. Since she wanted to remain at my parents' place in north Seattle, she jumped out of the car and refused to return. I followed her into a farm field and found her on the other side of an electric fence. I pleaded with her. She just yowled at me. Unfortunately, I couldn't wait for her to change her mind. I was in a hurry to meet a plane at the airport. It was a difficult choice between leaving my young son stranded at the airport or else leaving my cat on the other side of the electric fence in a neighbor's field next to my parents' home. Finally, I decided that Mildred could walk next door to my parents' home. So I left for the airport, planning to pick up the cat in a few hours.

Unfortunately, I never saw Mildred again. But that's not the end of this story. The cat apparently tried to find me. It showed up at my brother's home in Oregon some 300 miles away. I calculate that it followed familiar scents, magnetic attraction, or some sort of homing beacon due south along Highway I-5. Mildred's only mistake was not taking a hard left turn in Portland to find my home on Mount Hood. Of course, she'd never traveled this road to my Oregon home before.

So she just followed a path due south to Eugene. I had recently visited my brother there. My brother and Mildred knew each other very well. One day my brother called me to report that my cat had showed up at his house. Now many cats look alike, it's true. But Mildred was a twelve-pound, tortoise-shelled cat with distinctive markings. She also liked to bite people. When my brother opened the door one morning, this tortoise-shelled cat jumped up and bit him.

"Mildred!" he cried in disbelief.

The cat just followed him inside the house, as though she knew where she was going. Then she ran outdoors, as though she realized that it was the wrong house.

So when animal behaviorists tell me that cats lack the ability to visualize what is on the other side of a wall, I assume that they are only thinking of physical attributes. They must be ignoring the awareness of a cat. Awareness comes with a focused application of higher consciousness, something that cannot be measured physically.

Admittedly, I could learn a lot from my cats. They have showed me what is possible when you don't attempt to analyze everything and just trust your instincts. Our little brains get us into so many problems, including a sense of doubt. Catlike reactions, on the other hand, often come from a sense of confident awareness and focused intent.

Of course, I could also learn a lot from the dream master. Consequently, I made plans to visit him in the cavern again to resume the investigation that we had begun there. I meditated before putting myself to bed in a state of higher consciousness that led to another out-of-body experience. I held the image of seeing the dream master in that dimly lit cavern again, as darkness fell upon me and I felt my consciousness leave my body.

In a flash, I was back in the cave. The dream master stood in front of me with that customary grin on his round face. The cavern was still dimly lit, but I could see much better than before.

"And what would you like to know?" he asked me.

"You know," I said. "There's more here than what I am seeing."

"Yes, of course," he answered. "You are not seeing everything that is here."

I started to examine the walls again. I got very close to the stone surface, looking for cracks in the wall. When I could not find any, I moved to another wall. Soon I had circled the entire chamber.

"What have you learned?" the dream master asked me.

"That there is no distinct opening from this chamber that leads anywhere except back up the steps to the beach. This chamber apparently leads nowhere, despite the fact I have found air currents that seem to eke through cracks in the walls. But apparently there are no more chambers or passages beyond this space here."

"Are you certain?" he asked with a mischievous grin.

Somehow this made me feel uneasy again. I didn't want to appear foolish or indecisive, however. Really, I just wanted to trust my instincts and my new sense of awareness. On the other hand, I couldn't find any doorway to any rooms beyond this chamber. So I admitted to the obvious.

"There is nothing beyond this chamber as far as I can see," I told him.

"You don't sound very sure of yourself," he countered.

"Well, I sense that there is something else," I said, "but I am unable to find anything. So the evidence says that there is nothing else."

"Evidence!" he retorted. "You want evidence?"

"Well, yes," I said."

"What would satisfy you?"

"Finding an opening," I replied.

He walked over to one of the walls and started feeling everywhere, even peering into corners. He didn't seem very serious in this effort; so I thought that he was mocking my actions.

"Anything?" I asked.

"I am just checking your work," he said. "Very thorough, as far as it goes."

"Then I am missing something else?" I asked.

"Of course," he said. "Always trust your awareness."

"What else is there to check?" I asked.

"Well," he said thoughtfully, "did you think to look anywhere outside this room?"

This approach stopped me cold. I did not know how to respond to him. I did not know where he was going.

"No," I said finally in a small voice.

"You checked the immediate, physical evidence. Sometimes the answers lie behind the immediate, physical evidence. What you see, then, is the end result of something that occurs somewhere else. What you see in the end, therefore, makes very little sense to you."

"Because I am on the outside, looking in?" I asked.

"Or perhaps on the inside, looking out," he suggested. "It's all the same problem really."

I started to make circles in the dirt floor with my feet.

"So I can only experience the place where I am. Is that what you're telling me?" I asked.

"Not exactly," the dream master said. "Other possibilities unfold, when you are ready."

"How?" I asked.

"You unfold them," the dream master said.

"I can't do that," I told him.

"I know," he answered. "So I will help you."

"How do you unfold them?" I asked.

He chuckled. Then he looked at me seriously. He drew nearer to talk more intimately.

"I will unfold them in a way that seems right for you," he said. "Something you can relate to."

"Okay," I said. "I'm ready."

"So you want a show now?" he said. "Okay, I will give you a show."

The dream master turned sharply to face the wall to the left of us. To me, it looked identical to the other walls. He raised his right arm to the wall and then swooped his arm at a downward angle in one forceful movement.

The wall opened like an electronic gate that had been triggered to open on command. The stone wall folded inward from the right to the left.

The collapsing of the wall startled a man who sat in a chair on the other side of the wall. He was watching television! He turned to see us. For the longest time, he simply stared at us in disbelief.

"Hum?" the dream master said to me.

"Amazing!" I said.

"Wait," he said. "There's more."

He raised his arm again and aimed it in the direction of the man. Again, he swooped his arm downward.

The stone wall behind the man also folded from right to left, uncovering another room behind the chamber where the man sat.

Another man was seated in that room, positioned in a chair much like the first man. This man was also watching television and appeared startled to be uncovered by us.

My mouth dropped open; and I was totally speechless for the moment.

This seemed to delight the dream master. He started whooping with laughter and clapping his hands at the great unveiling. He even did a little dance in his sandals.

"Wait, there's more!" he said. And he raised his arm again. When his arm swooped down, the stone wall behind the second man folded open from right to left, exactly like the other walls.

Another man was seated in a chair in a position similar to the first two men. He was far from us and a bit hard to see, but I believe that he was watching television, too. When the wall opened, he turned toward us, exactly as the other two men had done.

The three men appeared identical in all ways and were perfectly aligned in a vertical row, as we watched them watching us. It was like looking at photocopies of the same thing, all perfectly aligned.

"Amazing!" I said again.

"Well, I thought that you would like it presented this way," he said. "There are many possible ways to look at it, of course."

Nine
The Initiation

THAT LAST LESSON in the cave reminded me of the time I had tried flying a plane through fog. I wasn't a licensed pilot or even an experienced student. That didn't stop me from trying to fly through fog blindly, however.

At the time, I was working for the *Ketchikan Daily News,* a newspaper in Alaska. As part of our monthly routine, the staff took turns visiting remote island communities to gather news and advertisements for a monthly regional magazine called the *Southeastern Log.* It just happened that my turn occurred during a late autumn fog.

Because I had been learning to fly in the bush, the pilot of our two-seater float plane gave me the stick, so that I could try my hand at dead-reckoning in fog. Eventually, Alaskan pilots must acquire some sense of this intuitive navigation. Most small planes, including ours, did not have instruments. Fog and other inclement weather is so common in Alaska that flight is often necessary on even bad flying days, since there is other way to get to remote islands other than by boat. Our newspaper didn't own such a boat, but did have access to this float plane. It did not use a normal runway, but instead made all takeoffs and landings in water.

Consequently, we were flying through dense morning fog, hoping to dead-reckon our way to the city harbor at Petersburg, Alaska. The pilot gave me the controls with the instructions to find the harbor by instinct.

"When you feel like you're over the harbor, take her down for a look," he told me.

This is what bush pilots in Alaska call flying by the seat of your pants. And it sounded like fun to me—sort of a game. All I had to do was discover a small patch of land in the middle of the ocean. Of course, we had a specific place in mind—the city harbor in Petersburg.

Now city harbors in Alaska can be busy places. This is especially true of islands where marine traffic is vital. Cargo ships, fishing boats, pleasure crafts, Coast Guard vessels, tourist ships, and sea planes all share these harbors. It's the only way to get to any island or off any island in Alaska. Of course, it's sometimes hard to predict how much traffic there will be at the city harbor. That's also true of the city floats in Petersburg, a lovely Norwegian fishing village and home of many wonderful Tlinget and Haida natives.

The fog and possible congestion didn't worry me, however. I flew this little plane through the fog until it felt like we were positioned just above the city marina.

"This feels right to me!" I yelled to the pilot over the roaring engine. (We had rolled the windows down in the cockpit to try to hear things on the ground below.)

"Well, if you feel like we're over it, drop one wing and start your descent for a closer look!" the pilot advised me.

I did as he advised me. I started to nose down for a closer inspection. We'd been flying pretty low to try to see and hear something on the ground below us through the fog, so we didn't have far to descend.

The fog parted in front of us. We were immediately over the harbor, as I had suspected. Unfortunately, we were bearing down hard on a state ferry just below us. People on the top deck of the ferry started to wave to us, but then covered their faces to brace for impact.

We'd come very close to hitting the state ferry in the harbor. Luckily, I pulled the plane up in time to avoid the crash. But it was frightening. I turned over the controls to the licensed pilot and never tried flying in Alaskan fog again.

Wandering in the dark is a lot like flying blind. You know something else is out there, but you have no way to tell just what it might be. Your immediate world is a very small place. Because you don't see all that clearly, you begin to make wild assumptions about what's beyond your vision.

We're like that pretty much all of the time. The dream master proved that to me. I could not tell what was behind the wall in his cavern by the sea. I couldn't begin to imagine. And since I could not, I reached the false conclusion—based on inconclusive evidence—that nothing existed beyond my field of vision.

Certainly, this lesson comes easier to some people. Some people just have more imagination and can see beyond the immediate, physical evidence. My Kirlian photography partner is like that. She can look into a mirror and imagine how longer hair would look on her. In her case, it's not really a question of imagining *if* her hair were longer or *when* her hair is longer. She can simply look into a mirror and see what it looks like longer. I know, because she has demonstrated this for me. I saw her hair suddenly longer in the mirror. You may call this mirror magic, if you like. For her, it's just looking beyond the immediate, physical reality. She knows that she can discover this reality, because she helps to shape it. The dream master knows it, too. And with his help, I might someday fully understand.

Returning to the dream master was my logical next move. There was so much to learn from him; and I couldn't imagine what direction he'd take me next.

So I made preparations for a lucid, out-of-body dream in a heightened state of consciousness. I meditated with intent and put myself on my back in my bed to await the adventure. In a flash, I found myself standing beside cliffs.

What a surprise awaited me! This time, I found myself in a strange, new place. Also, the dream master was nowhere in sight!

I began to wonder how this could have happened. I had focused on meeting the dream master. I had carried an image of the dream master with me, as my consciousness left my body. I also had intended to see him beside cliffs. Perhaps I should have been more specific in picturing the cliffs behind the beach at the Aegean Sea. Or perhaps this was another trick that he had arranged for me to embark on a new, personal adventure of discovery.

In any event, I found myself standing at the foot of a very steep mountain. It looked like Tibet or pictures that I had seen of Tibet. I looked around me to try to find the dream master or any clues as to his whereabouts. I saw and heard nothing. The place seemed very remote and deserted. I felt very alone.

The mountain loomed above me with no trail or obvious path. I wondered whether I should attempt to climb it. There didn't seem to be any other place to go. I had asked for cliffs; and I got them alright. These cliffs would provide me with some of the most daring climbing that I had ever imagined. And what was the point? What would I find if I climbed higher?

Without any sense of direction, I wandered along the base of the mountain for awhile, pondering my next move. It occurred to me that I was here for a purpose, although I could not easily determine what it was. Therefore, I decided to act purposefully. The obvious course of action would be to start climbing the mountain. So that's what I did. Unlike the cliffs by the Aegean, there was no trail to follow up these steep slopes. All I could do was start pulling myself up by grabbing whatever rocky edges and vegetation I could find. This was difficult climbing for a novice.

I had done a little climbing, but nothing this steep without easy toe holds. For a newspaper feature once, I photographed a bunch of serious rock-climbing students in action. They scaled this almost vertical cliff with rope and other equipment. I just hopped along beside them with my new tennis shoes, taking pictures along the way. It had never occurred to me that I should not be able to climb that cliff without gear and assistance. Nonetheless, I reached the top easily and looked down. Then I started to worry about coming down, of course, after my preoccupation with taking photographs ended with the afternoon sun.

Climbing this new cliff in my dream was much more difficult, however. There were no easy toe-holds. Also, I could not see well, since it was growing dark. Added to these problems was the fact that I was wandering through unfamiliar territory. Honestly, I didn't even know where I was going and felt certain that I wouldn't know my finish line once I reached it. I just kept climbing, because it seemed the right thing to do. Something deep inside me told me that I needed to climb to the top. Of course, I also assumed that I would find the dream master somewhere at the top, since I had not found him at the bottom.

In the middle of all of this arduous climbing, I must have grown tired and unable to continue. I felt myself snapping back into my physical body to end the dream early. This left me with an uneasy feeling, because the dream was unresolved. I felt that I had seen nothing and learned nothing from this experience. Worst of all, I had not talked with the dream master.

In recording the experience in my dream journal, I started to wonder whether my relationship with the dream master could be ending much the same way my relationship with Selina seemed to end. Perhaps my progress wasn't satisfactory to him. Certainly, I had been rather slow to grasp any of his teaching and still didn't have much understanding. It would be fair to say that I had been exposed to profound truths in nonordinary reality and felt shell-shocked from the assault upon my consciousness. The dream master had challenged the fundamental way that I looked at the nature of things; and I had not yet recovered from the shock of his dramatic demonstrations.

That's not to say that I was discouraged. Quite the contrary. I was anxious to return to whatever challenges lay ahead. If it meant climbing a mountain in the dark, then I would do that.

So I returned to the mountain the very next evening by putting myself into a controlled dream. Controlling the conditions that put me into a state of heightened consciousness for a lucid, out-of-body experience was something that I had become accustomed to arranging. Lack of control over my dream setting was something totally new, however. Once again, I found myself climbing that strange mountain in the dark, resuming my ascent from the exact spot where I had ended my last dream.

Climbing that rugged mountain was one of the toughest thing that I have ever tried to do. Nonetheless, I was determined to complete the climb and somehow get to the top. The more I climbed, however, the more difficult the task appeared. Then I realized that I had been lost on the mountain and not really advancing. That has to be one of the most disappointing realizations for anyone who attempts to climb a mountain. Climbers naturally assumed that a vertical ascent will bring them to the top. But climbing a mountain can be deceiving. For every foot you go up, you tend to go one or two feet to the side in order to work your way up a ragged precipice. That's pretty much how I was working my way up this strange peak in the dwindling light. I didn't understand why it was always dusk when I resumed my climb.

I must have returned to that mountain five nights in a row, attempting to make progress to the top in each successive dream. Finally, it occurred to me that I was moving sideways as much as I was moving up and sort of winding my way around the mountain. I was circling the mountain, with a different view of the top each night, as I rotated around the mountain in my meanderings.

In time, I came to a more level spot on the mountain where the ascent was not so steep. There I encountered heavy brush and trees, which made it even harder for me to navigate my way upward through the heavy forest. There was no trail to follow. I was becoming lost in my attempt to climb this mountain, which had looked so easy to navigate when I stood at the bottom.

I had been lost a couple of times in the woods before. Once was camping in the Cascade Mountains. The other time was during mushroom picking on Mount Hood.

I learned that heavy forest canopy can make it difficult to see where you are going in relationship to the mountain. You make logical assumptions that you think will bring you safely to your destination. Unfortunately, these assumptions often prove short-sighted. For instance, you assume that moving to higher elevation will lead you in the direction of the mountaintop and that moving to lower elevation will lead you to the bottom of the mountain. This is not always true, however. There are dips and valleys in mountains. Sometimes you have to go down to eventually go up.

In my dream, I was trying to fight off despair over my lack of progress up this rugged mountain and becoming tired. I thought about my previous experiences when I had been lost on a mountain. I tried to think what I did in each case to eventually find my way. Then I remembered something else—something really helpful.

Thinking about walks in the wilderness reminded me of a time when I attended Camp Indralaya on beautiful Orcas Island. It's a wonderful Theosophical campground located on many acres of pristine forest land along the bay.

On my first visit to the camp, I had overheard staff members telling other campers about a famous tree in the woods. It was supposed to have healing powers, if you could find it. Intrigued by this legend, I asked one of the resident camp managers where to find this tree. She simply pointed in one direction. Then she told me that it would be my challenge to find it. Perhaps she thought that would keep me occupied and out of trouble for several hours.

Anyway, I did look for the tree. I hiked in the direction where she had pointed, but found only a little dirt trail that led into the woods. The trail ascended into the high woods, but eventually descended into a lush, old grove of trees.

I walked and walked without knowing where to look or exactly what I was seeking. It occurred to me that I could walk endlessly without finding my tree, because I didn't know where it was or what it might look light. So I simply followed this simple, animal trail through the woods. The trail got very sketchy in places and even seemed to disappear in some sections of the woods. But I worked on finding the trail and staying with that trail.

Then I heard a little voice inside my head. It spoke very quietly and simply, like a child.

"Sometimes you have to get off the path to find the path," it told me.

Wow! I thought. Who said that? Was it my higher self? Was it my inner voice? What it my guardian angel or spirit guide?

I stopped dead in my tracks. Whatever the source, those words seemed to make great sense to me. At least, they fit my situation at the moment. Therefore, I decided that they were intended to advise me in my journey.

So I stepped off the trail and started wandering in the woods without any trail to guide me. I just walked where it seemed right to walk, without any particular direction in mind.

That's when I bumped into a giant tree. It was a magnificent, old tree. And it looked very healthy and happy there in the middle of this old forest.

The tree actually greeted me in a quiet, little voice. "Hello," it said to me. I realized from the voice that the tree had guided me here. It was the same voice that had directed me to leave the trail.

I put my arms around the tree and sent it all of my healing energy and love. The tree asked me to put my arms around it one more time. When I did that, I felt an immense rush of warm energy that the tree gave me. It was much more than anything I had given it.

That memory of the warm energy from the tree sustained me on my tiresome climb up this Tibetan mountain. It also gave me an idea. Maybe this was another instance when a person could only find the path by leaving the path. In this case, however, I had not been following any path. The heavy brush, rock structures, and trees made walking in any direction equally difficult.

Nonetheless, I decided to apply the advice of the wise, old tree from Orcas Island. I sidestepped to the left several paces and then started walking in whatever direction felt right to me, regardless of the terrain or previous navigational course settings. Spirit lead me.

As soon as I started following my spirit and stopped worrying about finding my way, a strange calmness came over me. No longer was I tired. No longer did I fret over finding my way. For the first time, I was walking easily and comfortably. It sounds a little odd to say this, but I needed to get out of my own way. I had been personally invested in attaining my goal and succeeding. This was not about ego or personal achievement. There was no contest here. This dream was about personal discovery. In such a quest, there is no time limit or stop watch. There is no checkered flag at the finish line. You can take as much time and effort in walking this path as you may require. It's really up to you. In my case, I simply decided to get out of my own way and let my inner spirit guide me. It's so simple, really.

Once I did this, I started to find my way. I took just a few steps in a strange, new direction and found a path. Honestly, it wasn't a very big path. In fact, I might have missed it entirely, if I had been looking for it.

But spirit found it for me. I gravitated toward that little path in the middle of nowhere and followed it like a magnet. It felt impossible for me to deviate from the path, once I put myself on it.

In no time at all, I reached the end of the path. The path had led me to a steep, hill that led straight up into the sky. I could see nothing at the top of the hill. I started to climb the dirt path, put found that I slipped and couldn't find my footing. So I moved a little to one side of the dirt path and grabbed ground vegetation to pull my way up the steep incline. The sturdy shrubs proved ideal. I hoisted myself up the hill and flung myself over the top of the embankment.

To my surprise, the path had led me to the opening of a cave! This cave looked much different than the cavern near the beach, however. There was no descent into this cave. There was a broad opening; and you could see fairly well in the small enclosure.

I stood in the entry and wondered whether I should investigate this cave. Something told me that my chosen path had led to this cave for good reason. Consequently, I felt that my journey had taken me directly to this cave for me to enter.

Still, I did not see the dream master. That made me question whether this cave was only a diversion and delaying me from finding him. I continued to stand in the broad entry to the cave and debate whether to enter.

Then I saw a man who was walking in the back of the cave. Apparently he had emerged from the side. The cave seemed to widen in the back or have side passages. In any event, the man was now centered in the back of the cave against the far wall. He didn't notice me at first, so I wondered whether I should approach him or acknowledge him in any way. Since I was a stranger, he might consider me an unwanted intruder to his remote setting. So I just stood there in the entrance to the cave and watched him for awhile.

The man was dressed in a sort of black robe with a hood on it. The hood covered his head, so that I could not see him well. The man also seemed to be looking at something in his hands, something that he carried with him, as he walked throughout the cave. He held it close to his face, to see it more clearly. I had the impression that he might be trying to read something. Because he had his back turned to me at a slight angle, I was unable to see exactly what he was doing.

I was beginning to feel a bit like a voyeur, secretly watching this man. It began to worry me that I would be spotted and ultimately embarrassed to be found there. And since I could see the man in the back of the cave, it should prove even easier for him to see me where I stood in the light at the entrance to the cave. Any moment now, he might turn my way and see me. Consequently, I felt an urge to leave, conflicted with a compulsion to investigate.

The conflicting feelings that I had about standing there and watching this strange man was more than I could handle comfortably. In an instant, I found myself suddenly back in my bedroom at the end of another dream. That always seems to happen when I feel threatened. I return immediately to the comfort of my more familiar body.

I bolted from the bed. This was like no other dream that I had ever experienced. I paced the room, thinking about the dream in great detail. I felt some frustration from not seeming to get anywhere that made sense to me. I had not returned to a place that I knew or particularly wanted to visit. Nor had I found the dream master. This was beginning to look like a neverending nightmare, more than a controlled dream.

After recording this latest effort to ascend the strange Tibetan mountain in my dream journal, I continued to pace the floor at home. I wondered what really disturbed me most about this latest series of dreams. It couldn't be the strange mountain setting, I decided, because I had found a path and reached a comfort level in following that path. It couldn't be my inability to find the dream master there, either, I decided, since I hadn't specifically intended to put myself face-to-face with my mentor. After all, I had willingly returned to the grueling challenge of scaling the mountain night after night with a sense of focused determination. No, I wanted to scale that mountain, because I sensed that something awaited me at the top.

What really disturbed me, I realized, was finding the strange man in the cave. I was not ready for him. Was I supposed to meet him? Something deep inside me told me that this was more than a chance meeting.

No, he was there for a purpose. I had found him purposely. We were supposed to meet.

Then I understood that the only thing that stood in my way was a fear of the unknown. Isn't that what usually halts our progress? Isn't that what stands in the way of personal discovery? Of course, I thought. Fear of the unknown had brought me back to the comfort of my bed.

I decided then that the black-hooded man in the mountain cave was part of my dreamscape. His presence in such a remote, exotic setting suggested that he might be living in higher consciousness on that mountain. He was different from the Greek people I had seen on the beach or the primitive people I had found at the bottom of the great canyon. This was nonphysical reality as much for him as for me. This was a magical encounter in a real sense.

This encounter could not be delayed. Of course, I needed to steady myself and prepare for the encounter. But this was an exercise of the spirit, so fear had no real place here. I needed to step forward. Certainly, I had come a long way up that mountain through tremendous obstacles, too far to be disappointed. The adventure could not end now.

Curiously, my mood rapidly changed to eager anticipation. I could not wait to return to the cave and meet the mysterious black-hooded man there. What was he holding? What was he doing there? Did he have something to tell me? Clearly, I was ready to return to that exact place and time.

My overwhelming curiosity and thirst for answers positioned me for my next out-of-body dream adventure. This time, I carefully held the picture of that cave with the hooded man inside, as I focused my intent to leave my body in a state of higher consciousness. I intended to return to the exact spot and situation that I had left in my last dream.

As soon as I closed my eyes and entered the dark void, my consciousness left my body. I found myself suddenly in the entrance to the cave. The black-hooded mystery man was still examining something in his hands at the back of the cave, with his back to me. Everything was exactly how I had left it.

Then the man turned around quickly. He looked right at me.

"Oh," he said. "Good."

"Hello?" I said quizzically.

The hooded man walked toward me. As he came into the light at the end of the cave, I could see that he held a clipboard. As he walked, he checked something off his list.

"Good, it's you," he said as he drew near.

It was the dream master.

"Oh, my gosh!" I said. "That was you all along."

"Naturally," he said. "I've been waiting for you. A little trouble?"

I started to laugh.

"We have work to do," he said. "Are you ready to begin?"

"Always," I said. "I'm always ready."

"Really!" he said with feigned shock.

I tried to get a look at his clipboard. He shielded it from me.

"Not yet," he said. "This is secret society stuff."

"How secret?" I asked.

He looked at me carefully.

"Well, I guess you can be trusted," he said. "But not just yet. We need to wait for the others."

I gave him a funny look.

"Others?" I asked.

"Just wait," he said. "Be patient. It's not easy getting here, you know."

A weak smile was all that I could muster.

The dream master pretty much ignored me then, walking around the cave and checking his clipboard. It was tempting to analyze what might be transpiring there in this remote corner of space and time, Instead, I decided not to think too much and just wait patiently. All things will become self-evident at the appropriate time, I told myself. Then I started to wonder when it might be appropriate. This made me anxious all over again.

So I decided to put myself in the corner near the cave entrance and wait there quietly without thinking much about anything. I continued to stand in a dark corner of the cave for quite awhile, as the dream master made ready. The quieter I became, the more I began to absorb impressions of the things around me. I sensed the importance of the cave as more than just a rustic dwelling in the side of the mountain. I sensed the urgency of the dream master. Somehow, this scenario was very important to him; and he wanted to make certain that everything was done properly. I also sensed impressions of other people who had been in that cave before us. They, too, had gone through some sort of important meeting in the cave, which impacted them greatly.

In absorbing all of the impressions around me, I felt a solidarity and comfort that I had not felt before, when I was only thinking about myself. I felt that I was about to join something bigger and become connected in some special way. It was an exhilarating feeling; and I just allowed the feeling to run through my body. This was so much better than personal anxiety.

Another person entered from the back of the cave, emerging from the side passage back there in the same way the dream master had entered earlier. This person wore a brown, hooded robe, whereas the dream master wore a black robe. Otherwise, their robes looked nearly identical. I could tell from this person's build and walk that it was most likely a man and not a woman. I could not be absolutely certain, however.

I watched this new person meet with the dream master at the back of the cave. This new person also carried a clipboard. The two of them seemed to be comparing their clipboards. They moved slowly and carefully with great deliberation. After conferring for some time, they began to nod their heads in some kind of agreement. Then they turned and began to walk toward me.

I had been cowering in the corner on the inside front of the cave. They walked in my general direction, but not directly at me. When they reached the front of the cave and were nearly outside in the moonlight, they stopped. They stood side by side with their clipboards in hand. The dream master in his black robe motioned for me to join them. He pointed to the ground directly in front of them as the place where he wanted me to stand.

As I reached my position, the man in the brown hooded robe handed something to me. It was a garment that he had folded neatly under his clipboard. When he extended it to me, it unfolded in front of me. It was a black hooded robe, similar to that worn by the dream master, except that it was thinner and less grand.

The man motioned for me to don the robe. I looked into his eyes and realized that I did not know this man. He was a complete stranger to me; and I did not feel anything even vaguely familiar about him. The dream master seemed to know him well, however. Together they worked as a team.

It was odd that they did not speak. The three of us were totally alone on the side of a very remote mountain. Why the silence, I wondered? Would they eventually tell me what's going on?

Once I had donned the robe and put the hood over my head, as instructed by hand signals, the two men checked their clipboards one more time. Then they looked at each other and nodded again.

When I started to ask a question, the dream master put one hand in front of my face to halt me. Then he put up one finger to indicate that I should wait silently just a minute.

We stood there without speaking or moving for some time. I looked into the face of the dream master, but he would not crack a smile this night. He was deadly serious for once.

Then the brown-robed man raised his eyebrows. He seemed to be looking at something behind me.

He motioned for me to move a little to the side. As I did this, I noticed that a young woman had taken a place beside me. She was already attired in a hooded robe. I noticed, however, that her robe was brown, like that of the dream master's associate. The robe was otherwise like mine in that it was thin and less grand than that of the dream master or his associate.

"Good," the dream master announced at last. "Now we can begin." He turned to the other man dressed in brown.

"Yes," the brown-robed man said. "We are all here at last." He looked again at his clipboard.

The dream master pointed to something on the other man's clipboard. As soon as he did this, the man in the brown hooded robe seemed ready to begin. He looked up at the young woman and me.

"You," he said, "are the new Gnostics."

I did not understand what he meant by this and looked at the dream master for quick clarification. The dream master just looked at me with a serious expression and then looked back at the man who was speaking.

"Both of you," he added. He looked down at his clipboard and then up at the young woman and me. Then he turned his gaze solely on me.

"You," he told me, "will work on the inside. The inside."

He turned his attention next to the young woman standing beside me.

"You," he told her, "will work on the outside. On the outside."

Then he reached forward and lifted the hood off the woman's head. Next he removed the hood from my head. No more words were spoken. No clarification was offered to us.

Oddly, I never looked into the face of the young woman who stood next to me. To this day, I do not know who she was. Obviously, however, we have much in common. Somewhere out there in this great world, she is attempting to carry out the arcane instruction of two hooded men in a remote cave. Wherever she is, I assume that she is attempting to do the same basic thing that I should be doing, only working from the outside.

Ten

Time Perception and Mastery

WHEN THAT LUCID dream ended there in the Tibetan mountain cave, I started thinking about the individuals who had been involved in the initiation ceremony. You might think that I would be concerned primarily with the lesson and new assignment that I had been given. Being human, however, my first thoughts were not about duty, but people.

These people were largely a mystery to me. Even the dream master had fooled me by his appearance and stern demeanor. He looked taller and more imposing than he had appeared to me in earlier encounters. Perhaps it was the hood on his robe that made him look taller. Or maybe the astral body was fluid to a degree, shaped by energy more than anything else. Certainly, it was different from the physical body. My impression was that a person's astral body could appear larger than the physical body.

The other people in this Tibetan cave were complete strangers to me. The other robed man, apparently an associate of the dream master, was someone that I had never encountered or had any feeling about. In fact, I did not feel connected to him in any way, except for the brief ceremony that he conducted for me and the young woman. That woman, also, was a complete mystery to me. My sideways glance in her direction told me that she was petite and short. Or at least that is the impression I had of her. She was quiet and demure. Unfortunately, I had not looked directly into her face. It is possible, I suppose, that she is somebody whom I know. From my perspective in that cave, however, it was impossible for me to tell.

Now our lives seemed to be running a parallel course. She had been given the same charge or mission as I had received. Apparently she would fulfill it in a different manner, however. She had been told to work on "the outside," while I was supposed to fulfill the same mission on "the inside."

Eventually, I began to focus on the mission that we had been given. What was it, really? I did not understand it. Also, I was not given the opportunity to ask for clarification. Somehow, that was the way the dream master and his associate seemed to want it. It seemed to me that they wanted us to determine what that mission was. It followed, therefore, that we would need to determine how to carry out that mission from the "inside" and the "outside."

Frankly, I wasn't sure what a "new Gnostic" was. I was supposed to be one now, so I thought that I had better gain some understanding of Gnosticism. In order to find what a new Gnostic would be, I first had to determine what an old Gnostic was. While this was pretty much virgin territory to me, I was able to find a body of empirical information on the subject of Gnostics and Gnosticism. I had heard the terms before, but had assumed that Gnostics were followers of an ancient religious sect, long since dead. That proved only partly true.

Curiously, I found that a relative, whom I have never met to this day, was actually one of the translators of the long-lost Gnostic gospels of the Nag Hammadi Library. These were books of an early-day group of mystics who had a serious falling out with the orthodox Christian church in the early days of Christianity. They avoided being fed to lions in the Roman games by declaring that they were not Christians, but Gnostics. Soon after that, the early Council of Churches expelled them from the Church.

Gnosticism sprang from mystic Judaism and Neo-Platonism. Early Gnostics sought to transcend the evils of this world and merge into what they called the All, which they saw as our destiny as light beings.

Consequently, one could make the case that ancient Greek philosopher Plato was one of the forerunners to Gnosticism. Later day Theosophists could be considered neo-Gnostic and certainly Neo-Platonism. All share a mystical orientation to creation, humanity, and their understanding of the nature of things.

Early Gnostics did not believe in a professional clergy. Nor did they view the creator as masculine. To the Gnostics, God was both masculine and feminine. Furthermore, they believed in a broad pantheon of heavenly angels who could dialogue with people. There were legions of angels of every description and rank.

Many Gnostics believed that Sophia, the goddess of wisdom, originally created humanity, breathing the divine spark of life into her children.

Many Gnostics saw the serpent in the Garden of Eden as good in offering knowledge to humanity, but saw God as malevolent and blind to humanity.

Gnostics believed in transcendence of the human spirit and reincarnation. They scorned commercialism, communities, and political involvement. What they offered was an ideal, radical alternative.

You can see Gnostic thought in many of our great writers, including Voltaire, Blake, Melville, Yeats, and others. Many even see traces of Gnostic thought in such modern writers as Philip K. Dick and Jack Kerouac.

Because the Gnostics were driven out of the early Church of Rome, they went underground and their numbers dwindled. Then, in 1945, the lost Gnostic gospels were discovered in Nag Hammadi in Upper Egypt, a place not far from where the Dead Sea Scrolls were unearthed about the same time.

The transpersonal psychologist Carl Jung was helpful in safeguarding the Gnostic gospels when they were discovered and helped put them into the hands of religious scholars for honest appraisal. They determined that many of the texts were written about the same time as the four gospels of the orthodox Christian Bible and just as authentic in their description of early Christian discussion. In fact, the early books shed new light on Judaism, as well as the roots of Christianity. Consequently, the lost books both supported and expanded the view of Christianity, as seen by early Christians in the first century.

The Gnostic gospels, however, show a more mystical side to the historical Jesus Christ and more of a matriarchal orientation in his early organization of followers. Key Gnostic gospels were written by women. Also, the lost books suggest that the key disciple during the time of Christ was probably Mary Magdalene.

Understanding this mystery religion had its reward for Gnosticism's idealistic followers. The Gnostics' Gospel of Thomas promised eternal life: "Whoever finds the interpretation of these sayings will not experience death."

Since the Holy Church of Rome outlawed Gnostics as heretics centuries ago, I did not expect to find anyone seriously practicing Gnosticism today. The dream master and his associate, however, initiated me and a young woman in a Tibetan cave as "the new Gnostics."

I hardly knew what to think about this. I didn't even know if I had been to Tibet. I just know that it looked like Tibet or photographs that I had seen of Tibet. Somehow climbing that mountain for hours and hours seemed real enough, though. The dream master and the others in that cave seemed serious enough, as well.

So I began to immerse myself in Gnostic writings. Fortunately, many of the classics have been translated and published. All of the lost scriptures found in upper Egypt in 1945 are readily available today in one collected volume, titled *The Nag Hammadi Library*. These texts have proved to be eye-openers for me. These long-lost, early books turn the traditional Bible upside down. Clearly, Jesus and many of his followers were mystics, according to these Gnostic accounts, much like Eastern mystics.

For me, trying to determine my role as a new Gnostic who works on the inside could take a lifetime. The assignment seemed a little like Selina's riddle. I was certain that it would take me a lifetime to begin to understand either of them. That would leave little time to work the assignment or extract the benefit from solving the riddle. Well, time was pretty much irrelevant in the realm of higher consciousness. And, as Selina had said, I could always try again.

I was anxious to meet with the dream master again. Of course, I was hopeful that he might explain the assignment that he had given me in the mountain cave. I had my doubts that he would make it that easy for me, as he usually preferred that I work things out myself. But I was hopeful that he would provide some clarity.

Perhaps I should have been more specific when I asked him for clarity or definition, so that I would have more time to actually work my assignment. When I left my body on my next controlled dream in higher consciousness, I carried with me the intent to ask the dream master for definition, clarity, and control over time.

I appeared in front of him instantly with these thoughts heavy on my mind. I was running these thoughts through my consciousness, so that I would not forget them. Definition, clarity, and time. That's what the dream master heard from me, as I appeared in front of him.

He met me on the beach in the Aegean. We were standing near the stairs that lead down into the cavern.

The dream master smiled at me broadly, as though glad that I had raised questions for him. He ushered me part of the way down the stairs, although we did not enter the cavern in the rocky bluffs. Instead, we sat on a lower stair.

"So," he said. "Clarity, definition, and time. Yes, I know that you are obsessed with time particularly. Like everyone else I have known on the earth, you want to get all that you can out of time, like a sponge that you can squeeze. And you want to see your reality with great clarity and definition."

I simply nodded my head, hoping for all of the answers to make my life simpler and richer.

"I will tell you," he said. "Of course, you already know. But I will help you to see these things with greater clarity and definition."

"Thank you," I said.

"It's simply a matter of perspective," the dream master said. "That's why it's hard for you to see the obvious."

I nodded again.

"You really need to remember all of this," he told me. "Do you think that you can do that?"

"Yes," I told him.

"Perhaps," he mused. "We will try."

The dream master fidgeted with a stick that he held in one hand and started drawing in the dirt upon the steps. It seemed to me that he didn't know where to begin or else was reluctant to open such a large topic.

"You can't leave in the middle of this dream," he told me. "If you do, you might not get the entire meaning. You'll need to stay with me."

"I'll try," I told him.

"Do more than try," he replied. "Do."

He looked up from his stick and looked directly at me.

"The first part of this lesson is that time is an illusion that you can control."

"Like a magician's trick?" I asked.

"No, just listen," he said.

"Time doesn't exist at all, except as a convenience to people in the physical world. People invented it to mark the passing of events."

The dream master reached down to pick up a thin stick on the step. He extended it for me to see plainly.

"People think of time like a straight line," he said, stroking the length of the stick. "They think that time starts at one point," he said, holding the stick now by both ends. "They think that it ends at another point, at the end of the straight line. But time is not straight and not a line. Events take just as long as necessary to evolve. In the great universe, things take shape and pass into various states of being. To simplify things, people say that they are born and then die. Things do not really work that way. There are great moments in our memories, of course. We take a picture of them and file them away in our consciousness as history, dating when they occurred."

I gave him a blank expression. He smiled.

"Well, what I'm saying to you is that things evolve over long periods or durations. You can't measure everything with a stop watch or a measuring stick. That would be human concept of time, which is short-sighted. Things take as long to transpire as they require. That's all."

I told him that I didn't feel that way and could actually experience time passing.

"Can you, really?" he said. "That's just your perception of it. Your perception becomes your reality. But it isn't necessarily everybody's reality. And on some level, it's not even your reality."

I looked puzzled. He dropped his stick and put a hand on my shoulder.

"When you are in this current state of heightened awareness," he said, "you do not experience this same minute-by-minute passage of time. When you leave the physical world of sensory perception and small thinking, you do not experience time in the same way at all."

"How then?" I asked.

He looked at me with a sly grin, as though I should know better to be toying with him.

"Here there is no past, present, or future, as you perceive of them in the physical world. Here your simple laws of physics do not apply. These petty laws apply only in the physical world, probably to keep people organized."

"But you are suggesting that we are wrong in this perception?"

"Of course. It's an illusion. You can make a moment last as long as you want, if you enter a pure state of heightened awareness. Your meetings with me—what you call dreams, take only seconds of your time in the physical world. Have you ever checked the alarm clock by your bed before and after you experience the dream state? You are actually gone a short time by this simple measurement, yet an entire day might appear to pass here in the dream world."

"Why would we need time, then, to be organized in the physical world?" I asked.

"Good question," he answered. "Good question. People are herd animals, don't you think? They have an agreed definition about the way things are. Young people are taught this social order. Then people spend a life conforming to this social order. When you enter heightened awareness and leave the physical body, however, you begin to think pure thoughts, higher thoughts. You become an individual thinker with a higher mind. You think outside the lines. You see that the lines that you thought were boundaries were never present at all.

"So we see that time is an illusion and that the past, present, and future can occur simultaneously. That means that you can access the past and future, of course, once you master space and time in higher consciousness. If you don't believe me, try stopping time. Practice it."

I asked him whether anyone in the physical world ever manipulates time.

"Of course," he said. "Look at the best athletes, the superstars. They have learned to slow down time at key moments, when it suits them. You can do that, too. Just stop your sensory overload, which distracts you, and change your perspective. Get into a state of heightened awareness while in your physical body, during a time of need. You can run a race and make the last few seconds seem to last longer just for you. Or you could rush into a burning building and rescue everyone in what onlookers perceive to be just a few seconds. All of this takes great practice, before you actually try it in your physical body, of course. You understand that much, don't you?"

I slowly nodded my head to indicate that I did, although it was clear that I was taking in too much too fast to really understand.

"Well, you can take these ideas home with you and reflect on them. You don't need to understand everything at once, you know."

I smiled, so that he could continue.

"There is really only the *now*," he told me. "Everything else is a collection of memories or future considerations. So you want to be totally conscious in the moment or the *now*. To experience timelessness, you need to focus on the moment at hand. You must become fully alert and clear-headed. Meditate. Learn to meditate almost anywhere or anytime. This is something that you do already to join me here in this state of heightened awareness. Where you go in this state and what you do is totally up to you. This makes you a free person. This is real freedom. Everyone wants freedom of some sort or another. This is what they really want, deep down."

I began to stare at him. He was really getting through to me now.

"So then we have the magic trick," he said. "Once you become a master of space and time, you can be in two places at once." He looked at me quickly, to judge my reaction. I believe that he expected me to be shocked.

"You mean like the way I am here with you now, but also home in my bed in my physical body?" I asked confidently.

"Something like that," he said. "You are beginning to get the feel of it. Also, since time is an illusion, you can be in two different places in two different times. Why not?"

I gave him a funny look.

"You don't think that those ancient people you met at the deep canyon exist in your world in your time, do you? That was a return to when you lived that life long ago, from normal human perception. But in a real sense, these people still exist. Timelines don't run dead ends. Nothing really ends. Nobody really dies." He stopped suddenly, as though he had said too much, too fast. He gauged my reaction.

Since I didn't seem to be reacting too badly, he continued.

"I might as well tell you all fourteen parts," he said. "At least these are the concepts that I wanted to introduce to you here."

"Fine," I said.

"In a state of higher consciousness," he said, "you reach heightened awareness. You can leave your body, as you have seen, and do many extraordinary things in this state. Some of these things you have explored already. Others, you have yet to experience and understand. You can project your astral body somewhere, independent of your physical body. You can view people and things remotely in this fashion. You can even heal by distance in your astral body or simply by sending your constructive thought forms in a state of heightened awareness. Also, you can explore exotic realms, some of which you have already seen. But there is so much more. There are realities within realities."

I was spellbound by the possibilities he offered to me. I wanted very much to remember every word of what he was telling me now and record it all exactly as spoken the minute I was back in my room with my journal.

The dream master seemed to sense my anticipation.

"You will remember everything I have told you," he said, "because these thoughts are etched now into your higher consciousness. Of course, it may be hard for you to write everything down in your journal, but you will know these things deep inside you, all the same. Believe me."

This made sense to me somehow, so I nodded my head.

"The important thing is that you are fully alert and fully conscious," he said. "Your higher faculties are engaged now. This is good. Back in your physical body, things are not always so good."

Yes, I felt totally alive and alert. I could think clearly in this state, outside my body. I must have smiled broadly or projected this sense of contentment, because the dream master laughed. But it was only a brief laugh, which he caught and stopped abruptly. He seemed driven to impart a lot of information to me at once.

"Clearly," he continued, "your physical universe is not the only universe or the only reality. There are dimensions beyond the simple dimensions that people normally experience through their sensory perception in the physical world. When people are able to leave their physical bodies through heightened consciousness, they can experience these worlds—if they can find them. Of course, they need a guide or mentor, as you have learned.

"Energy is all around us in all of these many universes and realities; and we can tap this energy to ride like waves on an ocean, if we are able. We can move through various scenes and great moments in time seemingly at will, if we can focus our intent and have sufficient awareness in higher consciousness. What we consider time and changing times are really energy waves that come our way sequentially. The energy waves differ, but most people do not recognize this. They lack real perception to see beyond the physically obvious. They pleasure their basic senses and assume that they are fully alive. Really, they experience sporadic moments in time, yet believe they are experiencing the fully flow of reality. You can see this now, can't you?" he asked me.

I nodded. Based on what he had showed me, it was impossible not to recognize this any longer. Still, I sensed that I had experienced only the fragment of the many realities that were available.

"You can understand this now," he continued," because you are becoming totally awake and alive. In your case, you had to put yourself into a controlled state of semi-sleep before you could become awake. You had to leave your physical body, before you could become fully alive. Isn't this ironic in a way?"

I shook my head to indicate that I agreed.

"Well, when you become completely awake and alive," the dream master said, " you can integrate your many bodies. You will feel everything around you with every essence of your being. You will sense the worlds around you and know the realities that lie beyond your immediate perception. You will become a fully conscious being, integrated with the greater whole."

I stopped him.

"The greater whole?" I asked.

"Everything," he explained. "You will not need to be in a room to know what that room holds. You will see without having someone turn on artificial light for you."

I started to droop in shame for my past shortcomings. He put a hand on my shoulder for support.

"It takes practice," he said. "You will learn as you go, if your eyes are truly open. Throw away your glasses and begin to see the way that you were intended to see."

Practice I could handle. Practice was good. It would take me years to throw away my glasses, however.

"Yes, you will need to practice for the rest of your life. You cannot become a master of space and time that easily. Nor should you expect to be able to do superhuman things with these abilities—at least in the physical universe. You might find practical applications in your mundane world. You can change your perception of time and enter higher consciousness anywhere, of course. In fact, you can stretch time whenever it suits you. Perhaps that will make you a hero someday. It's all up to you. But do use this newfound wisdom and your fledgling abilities with caution. It takes a lifetime or longer to master these abilities. You can't just turn them on like a water faucet, unless you are ready."

I told them that I was ready. At this point he laughed his deep belly laugh. Then he got serious again.

"Remember all that I have told you here," he told me sternly. All fourteen points. Write it down. Write it."

And then he disappeared. Everything there on the steps by the beach disappeared. I saw only blackness. Then I stumbled out of bed, aware that another long dream had ended.

This dream was so intense, in fact, that I was too tired to record anything in my journal right away. The message of the dream master was so vivid in my memory, however, that I felt certain that I would never forget a single thing that he had told me.

The next night I sat down to write in my dream journal. Everything was still clear in my memory, but now beginning to fade. Consequently, I sensed that I had better write it all down as soon as possible. Unfortunately, I was experiencing some difficulty. So I wrote down my memories of this last dream over two days.

The dream master had told me to write down all fourteen points of his last discussion. This seemed perfectly clear to me at the time of the dream and after the dream for the first day or so. Then I started to forget. It seems, in fact, that I forgot one point for every day that I waited before finally compiling my list of his points. I could only recall twelve points. They were:

1. Time is an illusion that you can control.
2. Past, present, and future occur simultaneously.
3. How top athletes manipulate time.
4. Being totally conscious in the moment or the *now*.
5. Being two places at once.
6. Astral projection, astral travel, distance healing, and exploring exotic realms.
7. Multiple universes, multiple realities, and additional dimensions.
8. Time energy waves.
9. Becoming totally awake and alive.
10. Stretching time whenever it suits you.
11. Practical applications of time manipulation.
12. Precautions for time manipulation.

I sensed that my list was incomplete, but it was the best list that I could assemble at this point. Attempts to return to the dream master to resume this same discussion about time and reality proved futile. I found that I could not carry this intent into a controlled, out-of-body dream. Either I would not carry the intent into the dream, or the dream master would not review the discussion.

It seemed that the master wanted me to deal with it on my own now. If I only remembered twelve points, then maybe only twelve points made sense to me. What I forgot are probably points I had not really grasped in the first place.

So I have captured the essence of the dream master's lesson to me as best I could. As he instructed, I have attempted to write the points of his discussion on time and reality. Apparently, this lesson was more universal and less personal than his other lessons, although all of his lessons seem in retrospect to apply to many people whom I know and the human condition in general.

The dream master's lessons on time and reality have been described in a book titled *Perfect Timing: Mastering Time Perception for Performance Excellence.* I hope that I was ready to write it, as he intended. I told him many times that I was ready when I was not. He usually laughed at me. But then he would assure me that I could always try again. It was something that Selina, my first guide and his great student, had told me, too.

Eleven

Selina and Kirlian Magic

I HAD NOT seen Selina, my first guide, in a long while. Another person might say that a long time had passed, but I no longer thought in those terms. The teachings of the dream master had convinced me that time was pretty much an illusion. If anything, time is fluid. It is the energy of opportunity that we can use to experience personal highlights, provided that we are sufficiently awake, alert, and aware to seize the moment.

Selina had introduced me to the dream master and told me that he had been her teacher as well. Consequently, this made Selina even more interesting to me, after my many lucid dreams with her old teacher.

When Selina rejected my third response to her riddle, she passed me off to the dream master with the implication that she would no longer serve as my guide. Once I started meeting with the dream master, I no longer sought Selina. Nor did I expect to see her again.

I knew that she had some sort of interest in me and my activities, however. This was especially true of my involvement with Kirlian photography. A friend and I had assembled a special camera with much help from her brother to conduct experiments into the bioplasma makeup of the known universe and electromagnetic energy.

Selina materialized out of thin air in the presence of both my Kirlian partner and my son when they joined me in the newspaper's darkroom to conduct Kirlian energy photography. That happened before I met the dream master and ceased my dream walks in the enchanted forest with Selina. I had not seen her myself since she passed me off to the dream mentor for training.

Even after that, however, people around me would claim that they had seen a woman of her description standing next to me briefly. She would appear and then disappear without warning. Sometimes these people would remark upon seeing this apparition and shyly ask me whether I knew anyone with this description. Always, the descriptions they gave matched my memory of Selina exactly. So I supposed that Selina was still watching after me to some extent and never really far from me. Personally, I had not seen Selina in a long while and saw no signs of her intervention in my daily life.

All of this changed one summer day when my Kirlian partner and I decided to try a new series of particularly difficult experiments that involved leaves. We had been fascinated by Semyon and Valentine Kirlian's unduplicated exposures of a phantom leaf that showed life energy in the shape of a leaf after it had been physically removed or separated. Nobody in the West at that time had been successful in replicating the missing leaf exposure, to our knowledge. That made us eager to try our hand at it.

My partner and I made a makeshift darkroom in a bathroom at her home in a park. She was the caretaker of a state park on the Columbia Gorge then. I recall that we dark-proofed her home's bathroom with layers of black plastic and checked to see that no light leaked through.

We worked as a team as scientifically as we could on this one experiment. She would find a leaf outside and bring it into the makeshift darkroom. Then I would make the exposure onto Kodak Ortho Tri-X sheet film, similar to the film paper used at that time by hospitals for X-rays. Then I would develop the sheet film in chemical developing trays, using tongs to handle the sheet film. When the sheet film had passed through all of the developing trays, my partner would flick on the lights and then record the effort. She would note the type of leaf, the length of the exposure, type of electrical burst, the developing time in the trays, and a description of the photographic result.

The first time we tried this phantom leaf exposure in the makeshift darkroom, we achieved no significant result. That is, the leaf that we had severed and exposed in the tabletop camera did not appear to have a phantom image surrounding it. My partner had selected a tree leaf and then snipped one side of the leaf. Of course, we had hoped to see a phantom image of energy that would outline the former shape of the leaf where removed. But there was no phantom image of the removed part of the leaf. So we tried again and again, using different leaves and different exposure times.

Then I discovered something that almost caused us to halt our activities that day. I reached into the box of sheet film and counted only three sheets of film left. We assumed that we would need to call an early halt to our experiments with phantom leaf images that day, once these three sheets of film were gone.

So we tried another exposure. Still, there was no phantom image. I reached into the box of film, expecting to find only two sheets of film left. I was surprised to find three sheets remaining, however. Assuming that I had somehow miscounted the first time, I pulled out another sheet of film for another test. This experiment also proved fruitless. So I reached into the box of film again, expecting to find only two pieces of film this time. Surprisingly, I found three sheets again.

Seven times I reached into that lightweight box of sheet film and found extra film that hadn't been present earlier when I checked. I kept remarking about this to my partner, who saw it as a golden opportunity to keep going. There was a magical quality to all of this.

Finally, my Kirlian partner got the bright idea to try a houseplant. She brought an entire, potted shamrock plant into the darkroom. I wondered why she had brought the entire plant with her. She told me that we had tried every possible variable in our experiment except a variation in the time of physical death for the severed leaf.

That consideration of timing corresponds with another "near-death" experiment by the Kirlians. In that test, they apparently electrocuted a person to near death (without injury) to measure changes during death conditions. So we tried the Kirlians' near-death approach with the phantom leaf exposure.

My Kirlian partner held on to a shamrock as the lights were darkened. Then she quickly plucked one of the three leaflets from the shamrock and slapped the abbreviated leaf between the electrode plates of the Kirlian camera.

It worked! We know it worked, because our shamrock seemed to show three leaflets on the film. The two shamrock leaflets that had not been severed looked different from the energy burst that showed the outline of the removed leaflet. Nonetheless, our shamrock showed the energy outline of three leaflets, true to the original condition of the physical plant.

The success seemed to hinge on the short amount of time between the physical separation of the shamrock's third leaflet and our measurement of its continuing energy burst. The life energy of the severed portion remained for only a limited amount of time.

The success also seemed to hinge on our mysterious supply of photo paper. We never ran out of sheet film until we achieved our goal. Honestly, it seemed that new sheets materialized in that box.

Once we achieved success with the shamrock photograph, I reached into our bottomless box of sheet film again—just out of curiosity. It was empty now.

Was that our lucky shamrock? Was the box special?

I also thought about Selina as we were cleaning our makeshift darkroom. I remembered that Selina had displayed interest in our Kirlian darkroom work before. In fact, she had been sighted by two people when we had operated the Kirlian camera earlier at the newspaper.

With her interest in these energy experiments, I found it easy to believe that she might have helped us a little with the extra film. Maybe she'd even given us the idea for using the shamrock plant in this manner. The idea did sort of come out of the thin air, without a lot of thought on our part.

After all, Selina was very concerned about leaves. Her riddle of the bird flying out of a seemingly dead tree still confused me. What did it mean? What was the significance?

I still did not know these things. I could not answer her riddle about life, death, birds, and trees. But as she told me, I could always try again.

Twelve
Practical Considerations

SINCE EXPERIENCING THIS series of lucid, out-of-body dreams, I have been reluctant to describe them to anyone. They were intensely personal. They explored my innermost thoughts and feelings and eventually defined my own, unique version of reality. Additionally, I was reluctant to share my dreams with anyone, because they felt sacred to me. I thought that the dream master didn't want these special moments that we shared to be publicized. I thought that Selina was also a very private and sacred creature. To turn their conversations with me into a commercial book, I thought, could desecrate them. That was the last thing that I would want to do in repayment for all of the kind and selfless efforts that they have made to shape my conscious awareness.

This fear of desecration comes from a personal worry that I might have transcribed something that they told me incorrectly or given the wrong impression about something that I experienced in these controlled dreams. That would be unintentional, of course. Nonetheless, my reaction to my lessons in a dream state are immediately suspect as limited to my understanding and ability to interpret reality through my own perception filters. These were, after all, only my dreams.

On the other hand, the conversations that I had with the dream master and Selina seem to cover universal themes that apply to many people.

Only the method of their teaching seemed to be designed especially for me. That is to say that they waited for me to pose a question and then answered it in a manner that had special meaning for me within my frame of reference or range of perception.

Also, the dream master and the guide, Selina, seem to be universal archetypes that other people can approach. Enough people have received instruction in dreams from teachers, guides, or classroom situations to warrant that impression. Of course, the dream master or guide in your dreams might look a little different to you than the way I have described my dream teachers. We all see with our own, unique perception. Nobody sees even primary colors in exactly the same way. Nobody describes a scene exactly the same way. Certainly, we all see differently—even when focused on the same object. The dream master that you encounter probably will be customized just for you. While dreams and dream teachers might be universal, exactly what you dream and how you experience it will be personalized for you. This is because your consciousness represents your own, unique spirit essence. We are all connected by consciousness and spirit, but individual in our focused intent, will, and perception.

Ultimately, the dream master revealed to me that he wanted me to share my conversations with him. They were not mine to jealously guard. They were gifts of the spirit. Gifts of spirit must be repaid in kind. The dream master encouraged me to keep a sort of journal, something that I was not particularly interested in doing in the beginning. Men just are not as good at recording their impressions and feelings, it seemed to me. Men don't keep diaries, as a rule. While I was a reporter, I wasn't good at keeping a journal—at least not in the beginning.

The dream master also told me to write his lesson about time and record every point that he had given me on that subject. (See chapter 10.) My impression is that he really wanted me to share this information broadly with people. I attempted to do that as faithfully as possible here and in another book. I regret that I lost two points in the dream master's fourteen-point lesson on time perception and mastery. I honestly do not believe that I understood these last two points and could not internalize the message. Or it is possible that I simply waited too long to record all of the points of his lesson in my dream journal. Immediate entries are ideal to capture the full details of each lucid dream.

In fact, anyone who wants to approach the dream master or a guide in controlled, out-of-body learning experiences similar to the ones that I have described should keep a dream journal from the very beginning. Record your very first attempts, even if you do not seem to make contact with the dream master or have learning experiences in your dreams. You might not even recognize or remember your first, brief encounters with the dream master, if you do not quickly record your dreams in a journal. This is because your first experiences in higher consciousness happen when you have not developed much awareness. Awareness comes with an exercise of higher consciousness.

The dream journal also will help you to analyze your technique and sharpen your approach to controlled dreaming in the beginning. Think of it as a laboratory record of your experiments in lucid dreaming. Then after you begin to experience your own conversations with the dream mentor, you will have a mechanism and procedure for faithfully recording your experiences. Whether you choose to interpret your dreams in your journal is your own affair. Personally, I would not recommend it, since these interpretations are best left to the higher mind and not the lower mind that is our analytical brain in the waking, physical body.

In my own experience, the dream master often encouraged me to remember and write about my dreams with him. I believe that he wanted me to become fully conscious of the message in the dreams on all levels of my being, including my physical self. Certainly, Selina as my guide went to great lengths to establish a carryover message from my dreams with her by helping me to see the same dreamscape butterfly, man, dog, or herself in my physical world.

The approach to controlled, lucid dreaming might vary from person to person, of course. I can only talk with conviction about the technique that has worked for me. (See the exercises in the next chapter.) To fully explore the dream world as a nonphysical reality, a person logically needs to enter a state of higher consciousness through meditation or self-hypnosis and then the leave body in an out-of-body experience. In this sense, one's higher mind leaves the physical body. Consequently, it makes sense to do this in a safe, reclining position. You can do this while lying on your back in a bed, as though you are going to sleep.

The difference between lucid, controlled dreaming and normal sleep is that you remain alert in a state of superconsciousness during controlled dreaming, with only your physical body falling asleep. When you become accustomed to approaching the dreamscape and meeting with the dream mentor, you might find that you approach this state even in normal sleep. Your higher consciousness will activate itself all on its own and leave your body. (Of course, it is also possible to enter out-of-body adventures in alternate reality without dreaming in this fashion, as mystics have done for years in deep meditation in a chair or other sitting position.)

Just wanting to leave the body in a state of higher consciousness won't get you very far, however. Even if you leave your body in this state, you will need to focus your intent on where you want to go and then project yourself there by an exercise of will. In short, it will require personal power. You must work to discover the magic within you and then develop your own power. Like everything else, it takes practice. Every time you show some progress, however, you will find the next experience much easier. This is similar to developing muscles. Pretty soon the muscles are trained and can operate almost automatically from memory.

Even if you can focus your intent and project yourself where you want to go by an exercise of will, you will still need a guide or dream master to assist you on your spiritual odyssey. After all, you will be traveling into unfamiliar places and exploring worlds within worlds. You can hardly know where you are going, what to find, or how to proceed in these very foreign surroundings.

To call a dream master or guide into your life, you must visualize having such a mentor at your side. You must leave your body in a state of higher consciousness with an image of a dream guide who meets you when you enter the void. When you call a dream guide, one will come. You must believe this, or the visualization will not work. It is important to focus your attention on this need, as well, employing the full, personal power of your will.

In effect, then, you call the dream guide forward or summon it magically. Believe in your personal magic and take possession of your personal power. You cannot hope to leave the confinement of your physical body and this physical world to explore the unseen realities without a sense of spirit. Let your spirit be free.

Once you establish contact with a dream master or guide, you will be asked questions. Your mentor will ask you what you want to know. Your mentor will not weight you down with ponderous lessons, but wait for you to set the pace for your own instruction. Don't be petty. Ask honest, important questions that matter a lot to you. The dream mentor will not tell you how to win the lottery. The dream mentor will explain the mysteries of the universe to you, however, if you care to know.

The dream mentor will go to great lengths to make things easier for you to comprehend on your level. The master will probably demonstrate the principle in a dramatic fashion. In my experience, the dream master and my guide acted as Thespians in acting out the lessons for me in somewhat humorous and exaggerated ways. Perhaps this was meant to make it easier for me to understand. Certainly it made the lessons more engaging with more impact. It also made the lessons easier to remember.

The dreamscape where these lessons take place is filled with real people. That's because these places are real. They might occur 5,000 years ago, as we keep time. Or they might occur in remote, exotic locations that are unknown to us. All realities occur simultaneously, the dream mentor seems to tell us. Our understanding of time is limited and inadequate, the master suggests.

Curiously, however, we do not always interact with the people that we might encounter in these dreamscapes. At least, that has been my experience. In my own experiences in lucid, out-of-body dreaming with the dream mentor, the people who occupy the cities, beaches, hillsides, and canyons do not ordinarily notice me or acknowledge me in any way. They do interact with the dream mentor, however.

I experienced some exceptions to this rule. I interacted with my dream master's associate and another dream student during an initiation ceremony on a cave on a mountain top. I also interacted with higher spiritual beings when I left my guide and explored higher realms of creation.

Perhaps it's incorrect to even call these dream sites *dreamscapes*. The dream master and my guide seemed to make every effort to convince me that these places were real locations. What made them seem particularly exotic to me, perhaps, was the fact that I was visiting them out-of-body in a state of heightened consciousness. Of course, they were also places that were not part of my mundane, physical life and so exotic in that sense.

The teaching of the dream mentor seems to be focused primarily on mysteries of the universe. The mentor teaches elementary truth about time, energy, perception, human growth potential, destiny, and life. The teaching is accelerated so that each dream seems to build upon the lessons of the last dream. At least that has been my experience. Once again, I suggest that the lessons will be customized for each person to dwell on mysteries that most perplex the individual dreamer. The dream mentor will nudge you into discovery, but expect you to pose the opening questions and resolve questions with assistance.

Certainly, there are some precautions to consider. First I would suggest that you pay close attention to what your dream mentor tells you. The dream mentor does not make idle conversation. Everything that is said matters a great deal. You should not chatter aimlessly about how much you love birds when your dream guide is showing you something meaningful with birds, as I did. Focus your attention. Gather your awareness.

Also, you should lean on the good sense and leadership of your dream guide in selecting your path of learning during dream teaching. Your guide knows the various paths far better than you. The dream guide knows which paths you are ready to explore. Once again, I use myself as a bad example. I pressured my dream guide, Selina, to take me to exotic worlds that I was not ready to encounter. I believe that this led to my estrangement from my guide, who was not comfortable taking me to such dangerous places.

Another thing to avoid during dream teaching is obsessing over things that have amazed you. Once you learn a lesson, be prepared to move on. When the dream master showed me how to perceive color, I wanted to spend the rest of the time just finding more colors. Also, I was reluctant to give up the magic bucket that the dream master had given me to learn how to perceive color. The bucket was only a device. And once I had learned how to perceive one color, it should have been obvious to me that the same approach would work in perceiving other colors. We are so easily amused! No wonder we learn so little that is new.

There is one precaution that I never really learned to observe in my teaching dreams with the dream mentor. I never learned to control my emotions, particularly fear. The biggest fear, perhaps, is fear of the unknown. You feel this as intense anxiety and uneasiness. It makes you quickly leave an uncomfortable situation. When I would encounter something that upset my stability, I would often leave the dream abruptly, returning to my physical body and normal consciousness.

Learning something about the mysteries of the universe and ourselves is bound to shake your confidence a bit. Your fragile sense of reality is shaken by almost everything the dream mentor reveals to you. This is unsettling. A perfectly human reaction is to avoid it all. But you cannot avoid truth. It keeps returning for consideration. Sooner or later, you will need to face truth.

You will retain all of the emotions that you have in your physical body when you leave your body in lucid dreaming. You will simply take them with you. Your emotional body travels with your astral body. If you travel beyond the astral plane or lower realms, you will need to travel in your mental body or causal body. In the highest realms, you will not experience emotions. In most realms, however, you will carry your emotional body with you.

This is not a bad thing at all. You will experience many things in a dream state emotionally, which is splendid and revealing. But you need to keep your emotions in check. Do not be swept away by your emotions. Let your higher consciousness be in control. Use your heightened awareness to focus your attention. Remain alert and attentive. Don't fold under pressure.

Some of the things that you experience in dream teaching might seen contradictory. "The truth is rare and seldom simple," as Judge Learned Hand once said. That certainly applies to dream lessons. It is probably best that you do not try to analyze the lessons in your dreams in normal consciousness, since the analytical mind or lower mind that we call our brains in physical reality cannot begin to grasp some of the concepts that you will learn in higher consciousness. I can attest to this personally, because some of my lessons on time, for instance, seem to be contradictory to my rational mind. Nothing your dream teacher tells you, however, will be false.

That is not to say that your dream teacher will not stretch your understanding. Your dream mentor will challenge your perception. Trust your perception. Your spirit will not mislead you. This is because your spirit is pure, sacred, and wants to grow.

You will soon see a pattern to your conversations with the dream mentor. One lesson leads logically to the next, approaching mysteries of life from new directions. To some people, dreams appear unconnected. But like a labyrinth that challenges you to find your own way with limited clues, your series of guided dreams eventually will lead you to understanding. All paths should lead to this sort of self-discovery. With a dream mentor who guides you in out-of-body, lucid dreams during heightened awareness, all of your dreams will lead you there eventually.

Your dreams, of course, are very personal. They are essentially about your self-discovery and spiritual growth. Consequently, you should treat them as sacred and personal. Do not chat about them with everyone, as you would gossip about the mundane matters of the day. Treat them respectfully, as you treat your dream teacher and your own spirit respectfully.

That is why the dream journal is such a good idea. Keep it like a private diary of your dreams, recording your innermost experiences. Just writing down the events of the dream will help you to remember a dream on all levels and observe the sequence of your dream lessons. Later, when you meditate on the dream lessons, maybe you will reach some broader understanding of their meanings. These conversations with the dream mentor are meant for you. They are not essentially about your friends or neighbors. The meaning is clear only for you.

In recording your guided dreams with a dream teacher, you will become comfortable with the teaching process. You will realize that the dream teacher is always waiting for you. Of course, you will need to specify that you want to meet with the dream teacher and where you want to meet. You do that by focusing your intent on meeting the dream teacher in a specific setting and powering your intent with your will. That puts you in the right place every time. It also puts the dream teacher directly in front of you the instant you arrive. Of course, if you don't specify, your spirit might take you somewhere it decides to go. Remember to include your guide.

Another constant in these guided, out-of-body dreams is that your dream mentor ordinarily will resume the last lesson upon your next meeting, even if you do not focus your intent on a specific question when you leave your body. The dream teacher might approach the same question from a totally different approach, but will continue to explore the mystery until you begin to show some understanding. The master is stretching your awareness and perception.

It might be necessary for the dream teacher to poke some fun at you, but that's primarily to shake your unrealistic pride, arrogance, and shallowness. The teacher in your dreams will need to shake your total vision of reality in order to help you grow. You must allow this rebuilding process to happen for the evolution of your soul, even though it seems to destroy your entire confidence in many things that you hold dear in the beginning. Remember that there are many realities and worlds within worlds; and the dream mentor can reveal the mysteries of all of them, if you cooperate as a good and patient student.

Your own conversations with the dream mentor can become an ongoing relationship, as long as you pose new questions and show interest in growth. Remember, your dream teacher will respond to you and your needs. In this sense, the dream teacher feeds your awareness. As you become more aware, you will discover major gaps in your knowledge. A lot of people with very little awareness, of course, possess a great deal of knowledge about certain things. But they do not really know much of anything. They do not know how the patterns of great puzzles fit together. They do not know their way through the labyrinth of life. They are not even faintly aware of the worlds within worlds and the realities that exist beyond this physical plane. Once you begin to really know and gain a certain amount of personal awareness, your dream mentor will be ready to assist you in adding to your true knowledge. The only knowledge worth having, of course, is truth.

You must indicate to your dream mentor or guide that you are ready. You do this by posing questions. You will not need to shout these questions out loud. You need to hold them in your consciousness and focus your intent on them. When you do this in the presence of a dream mentor, your questions will be answered.

Do not expect these questions to be answered simply or directly, however. The dream mentor will likely present an elaborate dramatization to respond to your query. If you pay close attention, you will receive your answer. The answer might not even appear like an answer to you at first. Not every helping hand looks the way we would imagine, as we grope our way in ignorance up cliffs, through confusing caves, and into dark woods. But rest assured that the dream mentor will enlighten you, if you ask the right questions and continue to put yourself in front of this teacher in your conscious dreams.

Thirteen

Exercises

YOU COULD PRACTICE some exercises to help you reach a state of heightened consciousness and meet with the dream mentor or guide in out-of-body, controlled dreams. The exercises listed below are steps that I have found particularly helpful to me in reaching the dream teacher on a nonordinary plane of reality. Most of your lessons in these out-of-body experiences will occur on the astral plane beyond the physical world. You will leave this reality in an astral body, taking your higher consciousness with you. No single exercise will necessarily put you in front of a dream teacher in an out-of-body state of higher consciousness. Each exercise will bring you closer to this goal, however. You will most likely need to execute the entire series of exercises to precision in order to reach the dream teacher on the astral plane. Practice.

Exercise for Reaching Higher Consciousness

You'll Need:
1. Straight-back, hard chair in quiet room.
2. Firm mattress, cot, or mat in a quiet room.
3. Loose-fitting clothing to avoid feeling restrained.
4. Shoes removed.
5. Solitude.

Directions:

Part 1

Remove your shoes and loosen any tight-fitting clothes, so that you are very relaxed. Sit in the chair in an erect position with your feet firmly on the ground.

Become very quiet and still. Close your eyes and allow your body to fall asleep, while your mind stays alert. First, concentrate on your hands growing numb. Then consciously make your arms fall asleep. Next make your feet grow tired and fall asleep. Make your legs grow numb. Then tell your upper body to fall asleep. Allow your heavy, tired head to rest. Will your entire body to go to sleep, while your mind stays very alert and totally focused on the moment.

Tune out all distractions outside you and still all chatter and internal dialogue within you. Consciously shut down your senses, closing the floodgate on sensory overload. You are not distracted by smells, sounds, sights, feeling, or taste. Stop thinking. Blank your mind about all concerns of the past and future. Allow your mind to clear itself and simply occupy the moment.

Part 2

Do this same exercise while reclining on your back on a firm mattress, cot, or pad upon the ground. Achieve a meditative state of higher consciousness. Stay mentally alert, despite the fact that the rest of your body is asleep.

Part 3

Enter a meditative state while sitting in a chair. Focus your attention to still your mind. Allow it to become clear of any thoughts or distractions. Enter a pure state of higher consciousness. While in this state, walk to a nearby bed or cot and assume a reclining position on your back, as achieved in Part 2. Continue to stay in this meditative state of superconsciousness.

Note: Were you able to still your inner mind and achieve a sense of physical detachment from your body and the outside world? In a state of meditation, the lower mind gives way to the higher mind of heightened consciousness. To make this transition, you must control sensory perception and tune out distractions. This includes external distractions, as well as internal distractions. Stop internal dialogue. Halt all thought. Reach a still point within yourself and experience the quiet of being in the moment. The object is to put you into a meditative state in order to reach higher consciousness. Once you reach higher consciousness, you can do many things that are not ordinarily possible in regular consciousness. You can escape the physical world and even leave your body behind, as we will see in the exercises that follow.

Focused Intent Exercise

Once you reach a state of higher consciousness, you will need to focus your attention. You focus your attention initially on what you want to think about or do in this state of superconsciousness. Once you do this, you can achieve heightened awareness, which is far better than the five senses that you have left behind as ordinary perception in the physical world. You will want to power your focused attention with intent and drive your intent with your will. This is your personal power. By reclaiming the magic of your personal power in this manner, you empower your spirit and higher mind to soar to places that are beyond the reach of any physically-bound person. Without doing this, you remain in a meditative state and explore the universal consciousness with your higher mind. This is fine, of course. But by adding focused intent and powering your intent with your will, you can become active in a state of heightened consciousness. You can even leave your body and go to specific places to do specific things.

You'll Need:
1. A firm bed, mat, or cot in a quiet room.
2. Shoes removed.
3. Comfortable clothing.

Directions:

Lie on your back on your firm bed, cot, or mat in a quiet room. Lights may be turned off or left on if not too bright (as you prefer). Remove your shoes and make certain that your clothing is loose and comfortable.

Close your eyes all the way or at least part way. Tune out all distractions around you and internally. Tune out all sensory perception. Still your inner mind. Clear your thoughts, so that there is no internal dialogue. Think of nothing. Forget about concerns of the day and plans for the future. This is not quiet time for thinking. This is quiet time for not thinking. Still the mind completely, so that you can meditate.

As the body becomes numb and begins to fall asleep, the higher mind becomes highly awake and alert. You are entering superconsciousness beyond normal brain activity in the physical body.

Focus your intent on leaving the body for an out-of-body experience in higher consciousness. Picture where you want to go, when you want to leave, and what you want to do. Direct your intent not only with focus, but also the energy of your will. Feel the power of your will generated from the abdominal area of your body. It will drive your intent to empower you on your journey.

Leaving-Your-Body Exercise

You are nearly ready to leave the body. This will enable you to engage in conscious dreaming that you control. You can send your body wherever you want to meet with dream teachers. The following exercise will familiarize you with what is involved in the separation of your consciousness and spirit from the physical body and the physical world.

You'll Need:
1. Firm bed, cot, or mat in a quiet room.
2. Shoes removed.
3. Comfortable clothing.

Directions:

Recline on your back on a firm bed, mat, or cot in a quiet room. Make certain that your shoes are removed and your clothes do not restrain you.

Reach a meditative state by consciously telling the body to become numb and go to sleep. Clear your mind. Tune out all outside distractions and internal dialogue. Consciously turn off your sensory perception. Still the inner mind. Your higher consciousness is becoming awake and alert.

Focus your intent on leaving the body, so that your higher mind and spirit can leave the physical world. Energize your intent with your will, as you become conscious of a driving force from your abdominal area to empower your intention.

Think where you want to go and what you want to see when you enter the astral realm of spirit.

Visualize your life force leaving your body. Some people leave from an area in their forehead. Others leave from an area in their stomach. Most people probably find it easiest and most comfortable to escape their body from their chest or abdomen. What seems most comfortable and reasonable to you? Choose the point in your body where you want your spirit and higher consciousness to escape your body to begin your out-of-body adventure. Concentrate on allowing yourself to leave from this point. If one place seems difficult to you, select another departure point.

Note: Did you leave your body? If so, did you simply hover over your bed without much sense of direction? Direction comes with a sense of focused intent, driven by power of your will. It will also require a guide or mentor to help you on your way in the mysterious worlds beyond our physical reality. If you achieved no success in attempts to leave the body, then continue to practice the steps outlined above. You might alter the point on your body that you select for leaving the body. The exercises that follow also will help you to achieve success.

Kaleidoscope Exercise

Making the huge leap from normal physical reality to an out-of-body experience in alternate realities of the astral realm and beyond is not easy. Even if you mediate correctly and reach heightened consciousness with focused intent to leave your body, you might encounter difficulty. This is because the physical body cautiously holds you back, and the lower mind jealously guards you.

Consequently, many people find it helpful to "trip" themselves into an altered state to spring their consciousness free of the tight grip of their physical bodies. The technique that I have always found most helpful (and safe) in this regard involves visualization of a kaleidoscope. This acts upon the inner eye or psychic sense. It trips the mind's lock on higher consciousness and releases the spirit from the body. In short, it's a trick to loosen the grip of the physical self. Try this exercise:

You'll Need:
1. Firm bed, cot, or mat in a quiet room.
2. Loose-fitting clothing, so that you are comfortable.
3. Shoes removed.
4. Light overhead in your face, as you lie on your back.

Directions:
Lie on your back with shoes removed and clothes loosened so that you are not restrained. Close your eyes part way. Consciously will your physical body to become numb and go to sleep, while keeping your mind awake and very alert. Put yourself into a meditative state by tuning out all external and internal distractions. Consciously shut down your sensory perception. Clear your mind. Think of nothing. Find that still point inside of you.

Let your higher mind assume control. Think of nothing but focusing on your meditation. Think of nothingness. Find the center of your being by focusing on nothingness in this still state.

Your higher consciousness and spirit are ready to leave your body. They are leaving through a point in your body. Focus on that part of the body. Perhaps it is a point in your chest or your stomach. Perhaps it is a point in your forehead or abdomen. You alone know what is the proper way for you to leave your body. Your body and lower mind surrender to your spirit to leave. Your higher consciousness is now in control. You are safe. You are ready to leave the physical world, with your sleeping body safely resting. You can leave and return when you are ready.

You focus your intent on where you will go and how you plan to leave. You put the power of your will behind this intent to energize your thoughts. You direct your will from a point in your abdomen.

Now with your eyes partly closed, begin to flutter your eyelashes in the light above you. Close your eyes all the way shut, and then flutter them open part way. Repeat this fluttering of the eyes rapidly. Stop for a moment with your eyes part way closed again. As you do this, focus your third-eye attention on the light. Visualize white light inside your head.

When the light appears to you to be perfectly white, then visualize the light turning green. The green may appear soft like limestone at first. Focus on the green and make it turn dark green. When the green is the color of deep green emeralds, then make it dissolve again into a medium green. You might flutter your eyes in rapid eye twitches to adjust your inner vision.

When the green color that you see inside your head becomes medium green, slowly switch it to yellow. You will slowly begin to see yellow. As you focus your attention with your third eye inside your head, you will make the yellow more distinct, until all that you see is radiant yellow.

When the yellow inside your head is almost overpowering, then switch the color to orange. Make the color turn into orange inside your head. First the orange that you see appears faint inside your head; but then it becomes a more distinct orange—a deeper orange, as you focus your attention upon it. Visualize a long, full field of deep orange that stretches in all directions.

Then slowly transform the orange field into a field of red. At first you see a faint red, but the red becomes deeper and more distinct as you focus your attention upon it, willing it to become intensely red. Eventually, you see a deep pool of red everywhere. It is a vibrant red and moves you deeply.

Now begin to twitch your eyes rapidly again to race through a kaleidoscope of vibrating colors, now that you have captured them inside your mind's eye. Visualize them in this sequence:

1. Yellow
2. Orange
3. Red

Continue this rotation of flashing, vibrating colors for a while—perhaps three consecutive rotations through the changing color chart. When you feel confident in your ability to control the colors inside your mind's eye, then transform the red that you visualize at the end of the color cycle into black. Make the deep red fade into black. All that you see is black. You remain fixated on the black.

The black is a beautiful, dark richness. It is the void. The void is the vast eternity of possibility out of which all things come. You are now entering the void. Feel comfort in the black void. Welcome your departure from this physical world into the void. You are about to leave your physical body and this physical reality for the infinite worlds beyond this mundane world.

Note: Did you see the kaleidoscope of colors and control the color wheel to change the colors with rapid eye movement? Did you see the red fade into blackness? Did you sense your consciousness leaving your physical body? The following exercise might help you leave your body, if you experienced problems.

Reverse Belly-Flop Exercise

If you were unable to leave your physical body after the last exercise, then this exercise might help you. In fact, you might do this in combination with the kaleidoscope exercise. If you do so, do this exercise first, followed by the kaleidoscope exercise. This exercise could enable you to achieve an out-of-body experience, however, without the kaleidoscope exercise.

You'll Need:
1. Firm bed, cot, or mat in a quiet room.
2. A rod, bar or broom handle positioned under the lower part of your back, where the spine meets the buttocks.
3. Loose-fitting clothing, so that you do not feel restrained.
4. Shoes removed.

Directions:
Meditate in the manner outlined above. Lie on your back with the bar or rod under the lower part of your back at the base of the spine. Consciously will your body to become numb and go to sleep, while your inner mind becomes very awake and alert. Consciously shut down your sensory perception. Tune out all external and internal distractions. Clear your mind. Find that still, quiet spot inside you. You are reaching superconsciousness, as your higher mind is activated.

Focus your intent on leaving your physical body and energize this thought with the power of your will. Visualize the energy leaving the abdominal area of your body to drive your intent. Plan to leave your physical body and expect your consciousness to vacate your physical body through a specific point in your body. Perhaps you will leave through your chest, forehead, stomach, or abdomen. Visualize your spirit essence leaving your body from that point.

Consciously flex the muscles in the cheeks of your buttocks to raise and drop your lower spine upon the rod or bar beneath your lower back. (*Caution:* Don't do this forcefully in a manner that might cause great discomfort or injury. All that is required here is a very gentle nudge to the lower part of the spine. Make certain that the rod or bar that you have selected can not injure you.)

If you are unable to lift your lower back in this manner by flexing the muscles of your buttocks, then raise your back up and down with your hands at each side of your body. Don't do this repeatedly. Do it once, and then wait for results. If that proves unsuccessful, try it again in a little while, as you continue to meditate, focus your attention, and visualize leaving your body.

If this proves unsuccessful in helping you to leave your body, try adding the kaleidoscope exercise at the end of your attempts to shock your spirit to evacuate your physical body with the gentle blow to the lower part of your back.

Exercise for Entering the Dark Void

The dark void that you are going to enter upon first leaving your physical body is not an empty place to fear, despite the description. Rather, it is the eternal womb out of which all things come. Out of darkness all things come. Your immediate reaction to entering the dark void might be fear, but only because you are unfamiliar with it and uncertain where it will lead you. Everything that is created and materializes originates in the void. The void is filled with destiny and magic.

If the void seems too dark to you, that is only because you have not learned to see properly. You must develop new perception beyond that of the five senses that guide you in your physical body. Outside your physical body, you will need to learn new skills of perception, relying now on awareness. Your higher consciousness possesses awareness, but you must develop it and practice using it as a new skill of observation. Your astral body, the body double that envelopes your physical body in a subtle way, has sensory skills that you will learn to develop in the spirit realm. These are new skills outside your normal frame of reference in the physical world and very different from the five senses that you are accustomed to using for observation.

Here is an exercise to familiarize you with what you will probably encounter in the dark void, as you first leave your physical body for the world of spirit and nonordinary reality.

You'll Need:
1. A firm bed, cot, or mat in a quiet room.
2. Loose-fitting clothing that will not cause you to feel constrained.
3. Shoes removed.
4. Light overhead.
5. A small rod, or broom handle under your lower spine.

Directions:

Meditate in the manner described above to reach a state of higher consciousness and heightened awareness. Recline on your back in a firm bed, mat, or cot in a quiet room with your shoes removed and comfortable clothing that do not make you feel restrained. Consciously will your physical body to become numb and go to sleep, while keeping your mind awake and alert. Shut down your sensory perception. Tune out all external and internal distraction. Clear your mind and reach a still point of pure quiet and solitude within you. Your higher consciousness is thus activated.

Focus your intent on leaving your body, energizing your thought with your will. Visualize your will center in the abdominal area of your body and project the energy of your will from this area to drive your thought form.

Focus your intent on the point of your body from which your spirit and higher consciousness will evacuate your physical body. What point is comfortable for you? Perhaps you will leave your body through the temple, stomach, chest, or abdomen. Visualize leaving from this point and do so.

If you have trouble leaving the body, try the reverse belly-flop exercise or kaleidoscope exercise outlined above to trip this evacuation by shocking your spirit temporarily out of its physical casement.

You may feel your nonphysical body ascending from the ground and rising above the room. Feel free to rise higher and leave the room, floating through the roof of your building into the sky overhead. You might look down upon the roof of this building, but do not feel afraid and retreat. You are safe below. You are safe above. Let your spirit rise higher and higher into the sky, unbound by the ground below.

You may experience difficulty in seeing where to go or how to get there. You are floundering in your first attempt. You must adjust your perception. You no longer have physical eyes, legs, ears, or fingers. You do have awareness, however. You must focus your attention. After all, this is a new reality. Absorb it. Embrace it. Become a part of it. See with your new eyes. Listen deep inside you. Reach out to all that is around you.

Focus your intent on where you want to go. Energize your thought form with the power of your will. Intend to go somewhere. Focus on this intent. Drive this intent with the power of your will.

Soon you will discover a new form of mobility and a new way to see things. You are taking your first steps out of body.

Note: The rod or bar under your lower back should not be necessary in the future, as you will remember the sensation and react as though the prompt were still present. In this exercise, did you encounter difficulty going anywhere after initially leaving your body? Did it feel a bit like dog-paddling around in circles aimlessly without really moving forward? Then the next exercise might help you.

Summoning a Guide or Mentor

Even if you could navigate your way through the dark void outside the physical body, you would need a proper guide or mentor on your spiritual journey. The many realities and worlds within worlds that you might encounter outside the physical realm will be totally unfamiliar to you. Even if you could find them, you would need expert assistance in order to relate to them properly. Guides and mentors are evolved beings who selflessly assist travelers in the spirit worlds. The only trick to getting this sort of professional help is to ask for it properly. You need to summon your guide or mentor to request help and ask the proper questions. The following exercise might get you started in your relationship with a personal dream guide or mentor:

You'll Need:
1. Firm mattress, mat, or cot to recline in a quiet room.
2. Clothes loosened, so that you do not feel restrained.
3. Shoes removed.

Directions:
Put yourself in a meditative state to reach higher consciousness by reclining on your back and tuning out all external and internal distractions. Shut down sensory intake. Consciously will your physical body to become numb and go to sleep, while keeping your mind awake and very alert. Clear your mind completely of all thought and internal dialogue. Concentrate only on meditating. Find a pure, still point deep within you. There is no past or future, only the now. Embrace the moment in its entirety. You are entering a state of heightened awareness, governed by your higher mind and spirit. Your lower mind and body willingly surrender to your higher mind and spirit, confident that you are safe in your great undertaking.

Focus your intent on leaving your physical body, energizing this thought form with the power of your will. Visualize the will center in the abdominal area of your body, as it projects its energy at your command.

Visualize the point on your sleeping body where your spirit and higher consciousness will evacuate the body. You could choose the temple, stomach, chest, or abdomen, for instance. Consciously leave the body from that point.

If you have difficulty leaving the body, recall the sensation of the rod or bar under your lower back and how it felt to trip you and shock your spirit to leave the body. If this still doesn't work, then try the kaleidoscope exercise to trip your spirit. Control the color of light within your head with rapid eye movements to where you see white light, then yellow light, then orange, then red, and finally black. Rapid, vibrating colors that lead to black bring you to the dark void beyond this physical world.

Feel yourself rising out of your body and ascending higher and higher. At first, you are disoriented, perhaps. You see only blackness in the void and have no mobility. You are just drifting higher and higher without direction.

So you focus yourself in this new spirit body. Your new perception is awareness. You become aware of your bearings and begin to stabilize yourself. You realize that your higher consciousness moves by thought form, energized by the power of your will.

But where will you go? What will you do? All of this is new to you and most unfamiliar. You reach out for help.

Reach out for a guide or mentor on this spiritual journey. Call for help. Visualize a teacher who will guide you on your adventure of self-discovery in these new realities and worlds within worlds.

Send out a thought form, calling for help. Visualize the help you need. Energize your thought form with the personal power of your will. Hold out your hand and wait, continuing to send this thought form. Visualize receiving help.

Your call will be answered. You will receive help. A spiritual traveler will come and take your hand to act as your guide or dream mentor on your journey into spirit. It is most important here that you maintain confidence and continue to project your thought form and visualize receiving help. Otherwise, your message will be garbled or broken.

When your spirit guide or dream mentor finally comes to take your hand, you will see everything more clearly and have an immense surge of new confidence. This helping hand will give you great assurance and comfort. Your guide or mentor will not seem like a stranger to you, but like an old friend that you can trust completely.

Your new teacher will take your hand directly and take you forward into the astral plane to begin your instruction and spiritual adventure into self-discovery. This is the greatest adventure that you will ever take.

Soon you will notice that your guide or mentor does not speak much to you. In fact, all communication is telepathic. Remember, you no longer have physical body for normal speech and hearing. But your astral body more than compensates for what you have left behind. You can project your thoughts and receive the projected thoughts of your dream teacher.

When your dream guide does speak to you, most likely it will be a question. Your teacher will ask what you want to know or what you what to discover. This begins a pattern that will continue in your relationship with the dream teacher, as long as your requests are worthy.

Do not request frivolous things. These spiritual travelers between the worlds will not entertain students with petty concerns. Your questions must advance your spiritual evolution and understanding of the nature of creation. Your dream teacher wants to help you understand who you are, how you relate to the rest of creation, and the complexity of creation. You will spend quality time in the presence of a dream teacher to learn important things to advance your understanding and help you evolve. Do not waste the opportunity with petty concerns, or your dream teacher will discontinue the relationship.

Pay close attention to everything that your dream mentor tells you and shows you. Everything will have a purpose and meaning. It will not be always easy to comprehend the meaning of what you have been taught, but meditation in a state of higher consciousness will help you discover meaning that is not readily apparent to you.

Later, you can meditate on your dream lessons without leaving your body. Let your higher mind interpret your lessons and put together the pieces for you.

Your lessons from the dream mentor might come in many parts, as your teacher works creatively to break down complexities for you. Let the show unfold.

Do not be distressed or nervous during these dream lessons. You are safe in the hands of your dream teacher. As long as you continue to ask the right questions, your dream mentor will always be there for you, holding your hand.

There are four cautions to keep in mind, when you begin your conversations with the dream mentor:

- Be confident.
- Be responsible.
- Be respectful.
- Be observant and attentive.

It is possible, of course, to reach a master or guide in the spirit world through deep meditation that does not include dreaming. All that's really required is the ability to leave the physical body to travel into nonphysical reality with focus and intent. Of course, you would need to summon a guide or mentor.

There are two valid reasons why controlled dreaming is ideal for such out-of-body meditations. The first reason is that many people traditionally have found dreams to be a natural way to learn insightful lessons. We seem to leave the body in our sleep all the time to learn deep things, although we don't always control our dreams or enter our dreams in a heightened state of awareness. Consequently, the body seems most willing to open the door to such exploration during our dreams—whether sleeping dreams or lucid, waking dreams.

The other reason why controlled dreaming is ideal for out-of-body meditations is that it's safe. Your physical body is comfortable tucked away in bed in a quiet room, while your higher consciousness takes your spirit on an out-of-body journey of discovery.

This journal outline should give you the starting steps to begin your own conversations with a dream teacher in out-of-body learning adventures. Practicing the exercises will help you to perfect your technique, if you are focused. And should you experience difficulties anywhere along your path, just remember the reassuring words of my guide, Selina: You can always try again.

Special Note to Readers

Perhaps you have had experiences similar to those described in this book. Have you received training from a dream master or guide while out of body in a state of heightened consciousness? If you would like to share these experiences for a possible sequel to this book, please write the author:

Von Braschler
c/o Llewellyn Publications
P.O. Box 64383, Dept. 0-7387-0250-1
St. Paul, MN 55164-0383 USA

Glossary

THE FOLLOWING ARE words and terms as used in this book.

Analytical Mind
The lower mind or mind associated with your physical body, used in rational decision-making and normal daily mental activity.

Astral Body
One's nonphysical body that immediately encases the physical body and is associated with astral realm functions in the reality that is immediately beyond the physical realm.

Astral Double
One's nonphysical body in the astral realm or one's astral body in assuming the energy from that subtle level of being.

Astral Projection
Projecting one's conscious energy to a location without physically visiting that location other than through consciousness.

Astral Realm

The nonphysical world or level of reality that is based on astral energy and immediately accessible from the nearby physical realm.

Astral Travel

Visiting the astral realm of nonphysical reality in one's astral body.

Awareness

One's perception outside of physical sensory perception in coming to sense things and know things on a deeper level of consciousness.

Centering

Gathering one's conscious attention deep inside oneself to focus on the still point at the center of being. This could be used as an approach for beginning to meditate.

Chakras

The swirling vortexes of energy or psychic force associated with strategic points on the human body. Each chakra is associated with a different color and function.

Chant

Human intonation with controlled breath, tonal quality, and conscious intent, that creates power from the tones and carries over great distances with mysterious effects.

Color Magic

Magical effects created from the use of color with focused intent and often used in conjunction with ceremonies and spells.

Conscious Awareness

Pure thought of the higher mind and understanding of things outside oneself and beyond the limitations of the physical or analytical mind.

Controlled Dreaming

Dreaming with focused intent in higher consciousness to reach a dreamscape outside ordinary reality for soul travel and spiritual self-discovery.

Delta Brain Wave

The normal, slower brain activity in regular sleep.

Deva

From Hindu spiritual tradition, a nature spirit or elemental energy.

Doppelganger

One's astral double in close proximity to one's physical body.

Dream Journal

A personal diary of one's spiritual adventures of self-discovery in controlled dreaming.

Dream Mentor

A spiritual traveler or evolved teacher who assists people in spiritual dreaming.

Focus

Riveting your attention on one thing only or in one direction without inclusion of any distraction.

Frame of Reference

One's unique framework of understanding based on personal references to past events and information that have shaped one's life.

Guide (Spiritual)

A spiritual traveler who assists persons on their journeys of self-discovery during a dream or soul travel into nonphysical realms of reality.

Heightened Consciousness

A level of attention and understanding of things around you that is reached only with the higher mind in a meditative state.

Higher Mind

The mind that is outside the self and reached in a focused, meditative state of higher consciousness in which the lower, analytical mind of the physical body is temporarily disconnected.

Kirlian Photography

Named for Russian scientists Semyon and Valentine Kirlian, this fixed camera process appears to record electrical field change of the human body or other living things directly onto film, after stimulation of the subject by high-frequency, high-voltage electricity.

Illusion

A false impression of what is actually seen. The Hindu concept of *maya* as a veil of confused mystery that shrouds human understanding in a way that must be overcome through spiritual understanding and evolution.

Imagery

Detailed shape and substance that you can give to your intense thought forms in a way that makes them come alive in a specific, intended way.

Intent (Magical)

Empowerment of your thoughts with focused energy so that they assume a specific form or direction of your personal choice. Also, the magical purpose behind something.

Lodestone

A grayish magnetite ore that naturally attracts iron.

Lucid Dreaming

Vivid dreams that are controlled, out-of-body, spiritual adventures into realms of self-discovery.

Master (Spiritual)

An evolved soul that elects to serve as a spiritual teacher to serious students, often on a nonphysical plane of existence.

Meditation

A controlled, quiet state of being where a person finds the still point within the self and turns off all possible distractions to enter a state of higher consciousness.

Mirror Magic

Real magic that involves the use of a mirror or mirrors.

Mundane World

The ordinary world of physical existence.

Out of Body

Existence outside the ordinary, physical reality or everyday world in which a person's consciousness or subtle body leaves the physical body for adventure and discovery.

Post-Hypnotic Suggestion

A powerful suggestion given to a subject under hypnosis to do or say something upon specific cue after returning from the hypnotic state.

Rapid Beta Brain Waves

Highly active brain activity, often during focused activity.

Regression

Causing a person to reflect deeply into the past through controlled hypnosis or personal therapy.

Self-Hypnosis

Entering a self-induced altered mind state through a series of steps and personally controlling the hypnotic experience.

Soul Travel

Out-of-body travel in which one's spirit body or subtle body separates from the physical body and embarks on a spiritual journey of self-discovery in various exotic realms of reality outside the physical world.

Spirit

The nonphysical realm of energy and pure consciousness outside our mundane, material existence. Also, the unifying explanation or matrix for all.

Subtle Bodies

The outer energy web or layer of energy bodies that surround the physical body and amplify it.

Supernatural

Outside of our known understanding of what is natural and common.

Tone

(*See* chant.) A specific intonation that has mysterious power in the delivery.

Visualize

(*See* imagery.) The conscious act of picturing a certain thing or event in your mind's eye and energizing your thoughts to make it actually materialize on some level of your reality.

Will (Magical)

An exercise of one's desire and intent by energizing one's thoughts with personal, magical purposefulness.

Index

Perfect Timing

*Mastering Time Perception
for Personal Excellence*

Von Braschler

How would you like to run faster, think more quickly, and project yourself instantly wherever you want to go? *Perfect Timing* incorporates scientific evidence that time is elastic and subject to our will and intent. In the realm where the limitations of physical laws do not apply, anyone can learn to astral project, heal at a distance, practice remote viewing, bilocate, meditate, and reach higher consciousness.

0-7387-0212-9, 6 x 9 in., illus. $14.95

Dreaming the Divine

Techniques for Sacred Sleep

Scott Cunningham

Sleep itself can be a spiritual act. During sleep we enter an alternate state of consciousness in which we're more easily approached by our goddesses and gods. Granted, some dreams do lack deep meaning, but others can lead you to higher states of awareness, provide comfort and counseling, and send warnings of the future.

Dreaming the Divine will show you a unique ritual system designed to secure dreams from your personal deities, based on the techniques of antiquity as well as on personal experience. It also gives you an in-depth guide to remembering and recording your dreams, interpreting them, and determining whether they're of divine origin. The techniques aren't complex—a few simple actions, an invocation, and a bed are all you need.

This book is no less than a guide to a unique form of personal spiritual practice. Based on three millennia of the continuous use of similar rites, it elevates sleep from a necessary period of mental and physical rest to a higher purpose.

1-56718-192-9, 260 pp., 5³⁄₁₆ x 8, illus.   **$9.95**

Spanish edition:
Sueños divinos
1-56718-154-6   **$9.95**

To order, call 1-877-NEW WRLD
Prices subject to change without notice

Dreams and What They Mean to You

Migene González-Wippler

Everyone dreams. Yet dreams are rarely taken seriously—they seem to be only a bizarre series of amusing or disturbing images that the mind creates for no particular purpose. Yet dreams, through a language of their own, contain essential information about ourselves which, if properly analyzed and understood, can change our lives. In this fascinating and well-written book, the author gives you all of the information needed to begin interpreting—even creating—your own dreams.

Dreams and What They Mean to You begins by exploring the nature of the human mind and consciousness, then discusses the results of the most recent scientific research on sleep and dreams. The author analyzes different types of dreams: telepathic, nightmares, sexual, and prophetic. In addition, there is an extensive dream dictionary which lists the meanings for a wide variety of dream images.

Most importantly, González-Wippler tells you how to practice creative dreaming—consciously controlling dreams as you sleep. Once a person learns to control his dreams, his horizons will expand and his chances of success will increase!

0-87542-288-8, 240 pp., mass market   **$4.99**

Spanish edition:
Sueños
1-56718-881-8   **$7.95**

Gypsy Dream Dictionary

Formerly Secrets of Gypsy
Dream Reading
Now Revised & Expanded

Raymond Buckland

The world of dreams is as fascinating as the world of the Gypsies themselves. The Gypsies carried their arcane wisdom and time-tested methods of dream interpretation around the world. Now Raymond Buckland, a descendant of the Romani Gypsies, reveals their fascinating methods. You will learn how to interpret the major symbols and main characters in your dreams to decipher what your subconscious is trying to tell you.

You will also discover how to direct your dreams through "lucid dreaming," the art of doing whatever you want in your dream, as you dream it! Practice astral projecting in your dreams . . . travel to new places or meet with friends at a predetermined location!

1-56718-090-6, 240 pp., 5³⁄₁₆ x 6 $7.95

To order, call 1-877-NEW WRLD
Prices subject to change without notice

How to Meet & Work with Spirit Guides

Ted Andrews

We often experience spirit contact in our lives but fail to recognize it for what it is. Now you can learn to access and attune to beings such as guardian angels, nature spirits and elementals, spirit totems, archangels, gods and goddesses—as well as family and friends after their physical death.

Contact with higher soul energies strengthens the will and enlightens the mind. Through a series of simple exercises, you can safely and gradually increase your awareness of spirits and your ability to identify them. You will learn to develop an intentional and directed contact with any number of spirit beings. Discover meditations to open up your subconscious. Learn which acupressure points effectively stimulate your intuitive faculties. Find out how to form a group for spirit work, use crystal balls, perform automatic writing, attune your aura for spirit contact, use sigils to contact the great archangels, and much more! Read *How to Meet and Work with Spirit Guides* and take your first steps through the corridors of life beyond the physical.

0-87542-008-7, 192 pp., mass market, illus. **$5.99**

Soul Mates
Understanding
Relationships Across Time

Richard Webster

The eternal question: how do you find your soul mate—that special, magical person with whom you have spent many previous incarnations? Popular metaphysical author Richard Webster explores every aspect of the soul mate phenomenon in his newest release.

The incredible soul mate connection allows you and your partner to progress even further with your souls' growth and development with each incarnation. *Soul Mates* begins by explaining reincarnation, karma, and the soul, and prepares you to attract your soul mate to you. After reading examples of soul mates from the author's own practice, and famous soul mates from history, you will learn how to recall your past lives. In addition, you will gain valuable tips on how to strengthen your relationship so it grows stronger and better as time goes by.

- Prepare physically, mentally, emotionally, and spiritually to meet your soul mate
- Learn to do your own past-life regression
- Read case histories of soul mates from the author's private hypnotherapy practice

1-56718-789-7, 216 pp., 6 x 9 $12.95

Spanish edition:
Almas Gemelas
0-7387-0063-0 $12.95

To order, call 1-877-NEW WRLD
Prices subject to change without notice

Spirit Guides &
Angel Guardians

Contact Your Invisible Helpers

Richard Webster

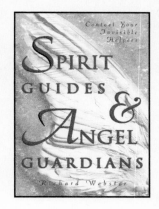

They come to our aid when we least expect it, and they disappear as soon as their work is done. Invisible helpers are available to all of us; in fact, we all regularly receive messages from our guardian angels and spirit guides but usually fail to recognize them. This book will help you to realize when this occurs. And when you carry out the exercises provided, you will be able to communicate freely with both your guardian angels and spirit guides.

You will see your spiritual and personal growth take a huge leap forward as soon as you welcome your angels and guides into your life. This book contains numerous case studies that show how angels have touched the lives of others, just like yourself. Experience more fun, happiness, and fulfillment than ever before. Other people will also notice the difference as you become calmer, more relaxed, and more loving than ever before.

- Learn the important differences between a guardian angel and a spirit guide
- Use your guardian angel to aid in healing yourself and others
- Find your life's purpose through your guardian angel

1-56718-795-1, 368 pp., 5³⁄₁₆ x 8   **$9.95**

Spanish edition:
Ángeles guardianes y guías espirituales
1-56718-786-2   **$12.95**

To order, call 1-877-NEW WRLD
Prices subject to change without notice